Demonic Torture to Spiritual Freedom

By

Tim Thompson

Demonic Torture to Spiritual Freedom

ISBN: 978-1-942451-16-7

Copyright © 2015 by Tim Thompson

Printed in the United States.

FOREWORD

This book is about a person living in a world of severe emotional, mental and demonic torment seeking love and acceptance from anyone even if they are into a lot of evil. Just knowing someone loves you, cares about you and just accepts you for who you are.

As this this young person grows up living their demonic hell inside of their mind it doesn't go away it just causes them to start to go insane. So many people don't realize that nobody has a goal or dream of wanting to end up in prison, mental institution, or wants to fall deep into the dark acts of evil.

Nobody wakes up one morning and says today is a good day to commit evil, wickedness or destroy someone's life. Each one of us no matter how bad things were when we were children, all of us had dreams and hopes. But through sin our direction, hopes and lives were changed.

So many think it's ok to dabble a little bit in sin but then realize that Satan took us down a road much further then we wanted to go all because we made that decision to dabble in sin. So many of us wake up one day and ask how did we get here, why is my life full of sadness and broken dreams?

So many ask why but sad fact is so many don't realize that Jesus Christ is right there waiting, just waiting for you to cry out and say "Jesus help me!"

For More Information Visit:

http://exposingthedarkness.com

and

http://pastortimthompson.com

DEDICATIONS

I want to personally and sincerely dedicate this book to my brother Paul for saving my life. I will always be deeply touched knowing that you lost your life to save mine. Thank you........

Thank you Lisa for being my best friend and thank you for all of our long talks about life. You have blessed me deeply.

Thank you Taryn for being my editor and taking care of my website. I can't put it into words just how much I am blessed to be your friend. I really appreciate knowing that you really do care.

Dr. Dean Helland thank you for encouraging me, being my dear friend and just being there when I need someone to either lean on or someone to go to for advice. My friendship with you means the world to me. You have shared so much with me, I can't say thank you enough for everything. I truly have always felt so honored just to hang out with you or just be-able to talk with you. Thank you.

Above all thank you Lord Jesus Christ for giving me a future, a hope, forgiveness, compassion, mercy, grace and thank you for accepting me into your arms. Knowing You as my Lord and Savior. When so many have found no value in me, You have lifted me up and have blessed me beyond measure. I am so deeply touched Jesus that you accepted a sinner as bad as me. You truly are so amazing!

CHAPTER 1

My story begins when I was 10; My brother and I were playing outside; it was a beautiful sunny day. He was two years older than me. We were riding our bikes up on a hill, looking at more hills and mountains because we lived in a small town where there were two prisons and a mental institution, plus one grocery store that sold food and clothes, plus we had 3 mini marts, all surrounded by miles and miles of mountains and lakes. Plus there was one, yes one, church in this town but very few speak about it or want anything to do with it because I have heard adults say that the pastor isn't in his right mind.

One afternoon, I will never forget this, my brother and I found a dead body, it was a female and she was badly beaten, raped and left for dead. My brother went down the hill to the nearest mini mart but he asked me to stay with this dead person, so I did. All of a sudden there were sirens and a group of police officers coming up the hill with their trucks and sirens going. The sheriff then suddenly showed up with his team and wanted to know what happened and who discovered the body. Then something very strange happened, the sheriff said, "This is out of the city so it is my instigation, so everyone leave". I could tell right away that he offended a lot of people and I heard some people say things that weren't nice at all about him.

But my brother and I were asked to stay which we did. We then saw this man coming up the hill and the sheriff said, "Hey boys, do you want to meet a great man of God? This is Pastor Bryon; he is a very powerful and insightful man of God". We met the pastor and he told my brother and me we need to come to his house for soda pop some time and all the candy we could eat.

After he introduced himself to us he went over to the dead woman and, as clear as day, I heard him say, "Oh how the weak must die and those that are weak and ugly must be given to the maggots of the earth". My brother and I had no idea what this pastor was saying but we watched them put a tarp over this woman and then they literally threw her in the back of a truck and drove away. The pastor and sheriff just stood there talking so my brother and I rode away on our bikes.

The next day my brother and I stopped by the pastor's house and he had so much candy and soda pop for us, it was like heaven. The pastor said, "How come you boys don't come to my church?" and I told him that my brother is very shy and I also told him that we don't have a dad so our mother is working all the time, so he offered to come and get us some time.

Within a short amount of time my brother and I were over at this pastor's house daily. Sometimes two or three times a day we would stop by or just hang out with him. Our mother was so pleased knowing we were learning about Jesus and as time went on he became like a dad to my brother and I.

As time went on this pastor began to share some very incredible secrets with my brother and I that he had learned from his own dreams. Like, I was so shocked that this loving pastor explained how Jesus wasn't a Jew at all, he had white skin, blue eyes, blond hair and loved those that were successful but had no use for the weak.

Then one day the pastor after knowing him for less than two years showed my brother and I his private office in his basement, he had these really cool flags called Swastikas and had so many guns in his office. He then showed us a poster that I never could understand, but he would laugh when I asked what does it mean, but in huge letters it says "Anti-government".

About a week after I turned 12, my brother and I were with the pastor's best friend going to the store, and a man who was drunk ran right into us and hit us head on. I don't know why but I am the only one that lived. I was in complete shock, nothing made sense anymore, and why did I live?

About two weeks later the pastor performed the funeral and I heard him say, "God allow me to take vengeance because of these deaths". That surprised me because I could tell the pastor was so angry I knew he wanted to hurt someone and make someone suffer because he was so hurt.

As time went on I started to realize that the white race was very important and how people need to protect it. Then to my shock the pastor said to me one day, "My young friend, so many question this or that, but loyalty is the only thing that deeply matters to the point of life".

When my pastor began teaching me how to shoot pistols and rifles, I felt so much love from this pastor.

About a year later I went to my pastor and I said, "I deeply miss my brother Paul and I dont know what to do", so he suggested that I write letters to him. But I thought about it and I thought since my brother is dead I need to die even if in a pretend way, so I climbed into a pretend coffin, lying there on a cold floor with a blanket up to my chest and I began to pretend that Paul and I were playing. At first nothing happened but by the second time I heard a voice. Yes, I couldn't believe it, I heard a voice from the other side, it actually said, "I love you and I desire for you to be close to me, God doesn't understand, nor care about you this is why he allowed your brother to die".

As time went on I began to experience severe nightmares, thoughts of suicide, plus I imagined dying all the time in many different ways. But no matter what, I kept going into my pretend coffin in search of my brother.

Then one day I heard my brother's voice tell me to listen to those that are speaking, they will become your friends and you will become powerful with them inside you. Well after I heard this I got up from my coffin that afternoon, looked in the mirror and said, "Voices from the other world, come all of you, come and live inside of me". Throughout the day I could hear voices speaking to me but I thought; wow, I have heard voices within but now I am actually hearing the voices speak to me with my own ears.

I went to my pastor and told him what I did and he said, "Listen and take notes because you are very gifted young man".

CHAPTER 2

I am 16 now, and my spirit guide is teaching me how to move objects and how to speak out things and realize that there's power in what I say.

My pastor got a hold of me and wanted me to meet some people that he thought would be great for me to talk to, so later that afternoon I said, "We will meet them". So I went and got into the shower and I could hear the bathroom door open but I didn't hear anyone and it scared me a little bit, so I hurried up and got out of the shower and as I walked over to the mirror, I literally saw on the mirror, "Redrum will be sweet to your tongue". It really bothered me seeing this because I had no idea what it meant.

Later that afternoon I met my pastor and he wanted me to meet some dear friends of his so we got into his car and drove for about an hour and then we arrived at this old abandoned looking house. Then on the other side of the house I saw that there were several hundred motor cycles.

A couple of people all dressed in jet black leather clothing came out and I knew right then and there that this was a motor cycle gang. One by one they showed my pastor respect and love.

Then this man called "The Snake" came out and gave my pastor a hug, then hugged me too. He said, "Pastor, I have a really awesome present for you, I want you to have it, it is a silencer, you can shoot this pistol with no sound at all". My pastor said to Snake, "Follow me". So as they were talking in private my pastor said, "You come too, my young son", I felt so loved and honored to have someone call me son.

The pastor then said, "Snake, I know you have been shot in the leg and in the stomach before and you have taken several risks for me but I need you to get Tony the hit man and let him know that he needs to come over to the house and have dinner soon and take my sawed off shotgun and take out some trouble makers for me". The Snake told Pastor I will send him right away.

Then The Snake said to me, "You want to check out our bikes, they are fast and we have fun because we are all family". Well for the first time ever I felt loved by so many and my pastor said, "Why don't you stay the night and I will call your mom and let her know you are with me", so I said, "Great".

One of the bigger guys called "Little Mike" came over and said, "Pastor, I want to show this young man that we have fun", so the pastor said, "Goodbye till tomorrow". Little Mike said, "Get on my bike and let's go." It sounded like one big roar as several of these people got on their bikes, went down this trail to the lake and there was a big fire and they were barbecuing. Then I was asked by this guy named "Squeaky" if I would like a beer, I didn't know what to say since I had never drank before. I enjoyed that a lot.

Then I met this beautiful chick who was known as "Flower", she came over and started talking to me, pretty soon I felt as if I was falling in love. She then said, "Let's get high", so we ended up getting high from pot and then before I knew it I was having sex in a sleeping bag with her. As we were doing it I was shocked, she was biting me and then she slit her hand a little bit and was whispering something all while we were having sex. In some ways it was exciting but in other ways it was very creepy to me.

Then we got up and started feeling hungry, so we got some food. It was incredible, this guy started walking down the path from the bikes where the barbecue was and everyone stopped and said, "Here comes Evil at its finest". I was shocked because I even knew that was not a good word to call someone, but as he got closer I could tell he was evil. He walked up to me and said, "Hi, you must be the pastor's son, I hear so much about you, thank you for being here with us, it's not often we can be around one of the pastor's soldiers".

Then he said, "My name is Evil because as time goes by you will understand that with trash you sometimes must use brutality and sometimes just a plain simple axe seems to fix a problem. I see you met my niece, Flower, she's yours now but I will take care of her till you are old enough to decide if you want her or not".

As the moon rose and it got late I was starting to get tired but Evil handed me a pill to wake me up and then he said in a loud voice, "Prepare the way for the spirits to arise", so about 10 people walked up to the fire and threw some type of oil on it and it got really big then and people were starting to eat this horrible thing called "Mushrooms", so I ate some too.

Then this woman ran up to the fire and said, "Oh Lucifer, we can feel your presence and I want you to take me". I heard it as clear as day, something in the fire said, "Then come and join me", so she jumped in the fire and I thought someone "Rescue her" but right then and there Evil spoke in a weird strange voice saying, "Our dear friend Liza gave herself as a sacrifice to the great and mighty lord". Well after that so many began to chant and I felt terror and extreme fear come over me but then, Flower, my girlfriend, said, "Are you ok? Don't fear the beast, he will speak through someone and we will all learn".

Then a woman began to act like a snake and started speaking things out that she was seeing and it just amazed me because I have never met anyone that saw the future, then she said, "You dont know me" and looked right at me and said, "I am the dragon and as you begin to know me and worship me I will hand you over anything you want or desire". Just then I saw like a ghost of my brother and it said to me, "Trust the dragon", then everything went silent and Evil walked over to me and said, "Tell no one what you heard or saw because I am the only person the great dragon has ever talked to, so this, my young friend, is exciting".

Then he pulled out a gun and shot the woman in the back of the head and her brains were all over, then he said she had to die because her destiny was now complete because she was used to have the great dragon speak through her. He then said to three people, "Hurry and go and get me spoons". He told everyone to just sit and chant, so we did. Then he stood up and said, "Oh great dragon, thank you for this feast" and each person was given a spoon and they cut the woman's head off and walked around with her head and one person at a time took a spoonful of her brains and ate it and then when you couldn't get any on your spoon there was another person that would cut a small piece of her brain out and put it on your spoon.

As the night went on I felt like none of this was really happening and I was in shock, but then Flower said, "Let's have more fun", so we ended up having sex again and again and each time she would cut herself somewhere and have the blood touch me, then she would lick it off.

The next morning I felt like someone had punched me in the stomach, I was so hungry and I wasn't sure what really did happen last night. Flower gave me a kiss and said, "Goodbye, till I see you again", then she got on her bike and went back to the house

This guy named "Little John" said, "Let's go get something to eat and then I will take you home", so I jumped on his bike and as we were going through this old highway, this small looking diner was open, Little John said, "I told you I would take you for something to eat", so we walked in and I couldn't understand how this place could be open since I knew it was boarded up and had closed a long time ago. How could a restaurant that was boarded up be opened again and I never heard anything about it anywhere?

As I was waiting for my food, it was so odd hearing voices in the walls crying out asking for mercy. I don't ever want to go in there again.

I finally made it back home and I was so glad. I was sitting there questioning what really did happen last night? Was it just a bad dream or did something evil really happen last night?

I found a note from my mom; she took a second job working at the bar for extra money.

I decided to just take a shower, I was so tired. After I got out of the shower and grabbed my towel and when I looked in the mirror I saw the words, "I saw what you did last night and I am watching you". I was terrified and I just wanted to pee and almost fell over.

I went into my pretend coffin and got the blanket just right up to my chest and started to seek my brother. All of a sudden I saw an image of Flower, she looked just like a vampire, and she said, "I am watching you", I immediately got up and just wanted to run but I thought where to so? I got something to eat and took a nap. As I was sleeping I had a bizarre dream that Flower bit my throat with her sharp fangs, because she looked just like a vampire, then I looked at the palm of my hand and it had a pentagram burned in it, then I saw her hiss and growl at me, so in terror I woke up.

Later that day my mom called me and said, "I am going to the city tonight, ok, so I will be home late". As I was just sitting there alone, I saw a shadow of a man come through the walls, and I saw it as clear as day, he just stood there looking at me, but I felt so much terror that I was literally paralyzed with fear to where I couldn't scream or even say a word, then he just walked back into the wall. I felt I just needed sleep, so I fell asleep and woke up the next day feeling great.

CHAPTER 3

The next day I got hold of my pastor and he said come over, so I went to his house and he said, "Did you hear that two more churches are going to be coming to town, and I just wonder if I should share some ideas on how they should be built because one thing I have learned is that after people start to realize that this isn't just a dead town, that things are very active here, most want to leave, so I will end up wanting to buy one of those empty churches". I didn't know what my pastor was saying, so just thought he was tired or wanting to imagine that things were more active than they really were.

My pastor said, "I have got to show you this", so he pulled out a Revolver and said, "Here, I want you to have this", I was so shocked because no one had ever given me such a wonderful gift, but then he said, "You can't tell your mom, and you must keep it here, ok, but it is yours". I said, "Cool"

I said, "Then so what do you use just in case of a home invasion?" He just smiled at me and said, "My young friend, as you grow in the knowledge of evil you will soon discover that what so many claim will destroy you are actually wanting to be your friend and help you".

Then he said something really surprising to me, he pointed out that cults or occults aren't evil, they are there because someone has decided that they are tired of the world, the government and the "so called" church telling people how to live. So now instead of everyone doing their own thing they now work together for the greater good. He then said, "I know you hear them, don't be afraid, just invite them inside".

That night, the pastor said "I called your mom and let her know I needed your help, so she just said to tell you that you can spend the night".

As the pastor and his wife were watching this mega church pastor speaking on the TV, the pastor's wife said, "Young man, be aware of those that tell you that the bible says this or that and they are full of rules. But this pastor on the TV he doesn't want anyone feeling bad or feeling sad so he preaches just happy things, that is what more should teach about. Look at the wealth he has; see, so many think God wants people to obey this rule or that rule, but those "so called" pastors are just weak and they won't listen. This pastor on the TV, my friend, he listens to the voices and they tell him what to preach, so he does it and people adore him".

My pastor then said, "Yes, it's true; the spirits are speaking but too many are cowards so they are bound by fear, claiming that they are not real so our father, the god of this world, just laughs because they are so weak and easily deceived. But our father blesses them with scraps of this or that so they will become lazy and complacent".

Well I decided to go home, so I did. On the way home I knew someone was following me but I couldn't see them. I made it home and I heard a loud bang in my room, I was so scared so I decided to go in there but I saw nothing, but I looked at my mirror and it said, "I know what you did last night, you can't hide from me". I felt such a terror come over me so I just went in the living room and turned on the TV and turned all the lights on in the living room and kitchen. I could hear voices telling me "That evil is arising, evil lives, and they are watching me".

All of a sudden I heard my mom's car, she came in and I ran up to her and gave her a big hug and said, "You need to see this", so I pulled her into my room to see my mirror but it was spotless and my whole room was spotless. My mom just kept telling me how proud of me she was for cleaning my whole entire room but I was just speechless. I was so scared but then I remembered what my pastor's wife said, maybe these spirits that tell the pastor on TV what to preach about are truly trying to help me in life.

My mom said she met this pastor who was up here who is going to have his church built up here. She said you need to meet him he is so nice.

CHAPTER 4

The next day I saw them breaking the ground and several people walking around up there, so I went up there to meet the pastor. I asked this guy standing there with a shovel, "Do you know who the pastor is?" He said, "Hold on just one second", so he yelled, "Pastor Mike, this man wants to meet you", so he walked up to me and said, "Hi I am Pastor Mike, I am so excited about this church being built here, and so what is your name?" I said, "Rick", he then said, It is nice to meet you". Then he said to me, "Even my bishop should be up here soon so will you be up here?" I said, "Yes, I only live about two blocks away from here".

Just then one of the bulldozers quit working and the guy yelled out and said, "Not again!" Then one of the trucks blew an engine. Pastor Mike said, "I don't mean to be rude but I need to figure out what is going on".

Well as the days went on I kept watching more and more guys getting all upset because their trucks, heavy equipment and tools just keep breaking down or were breaking.

The pastor called me and I finally said, "Since there are more pastors coming into the area what is your real name?" And he just said, "My young friend, I thought you knew my name is Pastor Ted". He then went on to say, "That church that pastor is growing will never stand or last", so I said, "Why? That doesn't make sense", then he said, "My young friend, that piece of property is very beautiful and very nice but it belongs to the voices, see, a woman and child were both shot in the head on that property right at gun point and they were kidnapped right from a day care center 45 miles away. The police then got into a very intense car chase with this guy and they finally caught up to the guy who said, "The voices said to kill both of them", so he pulled out a gun and killed them both for no real reason. It was very sad but when the voices speak we just know the walls, the ground, and the dark have eyes to see, and from time to time they even leave messages on the mirror for you".

The pastor had to go and meet some people so I decided to ride my bike to the land where they are trying to build the church and I saw Pastor Mike, he said, "Hi", so I went over to him and I asked, "Are things getting better?" He said, "No, and as crazy as it sounds, I am losing employees because they are claiming the ground is whispering to them to leave, so they just left and said I am not coming back". I said, "The ground does whisper", but he just said, "Young man, what you see is all there is, there is no other world, there are no angels, demons, ghosts, spirits or voices, there is nothing out there".

Well I was shocked because this pastor claimed it was all in a person's head and that the mind can play tricks at any time but I know what I saw wasn't in my head so why would this pastor believe this stuff? I left because I knew this pastor was sadly mistaken and I went home.

I wanted to go and see my new friends, the motor cycle gang, so I got hold of Pastor Ted and told him I want to see my new friends again but he said, "I wanted to know what you were up to." So I told him I was talking to that other pastor and how he claimed there's nothing from the other side, so Pastor Ted said, "Let's pray for him and let's go and see him. I will be right there to pick you up". I got ready and Pastor Ted honked his car horn and we went over to see the other pastor. I introduced Pastor Ted to Pastor Mike and Pastor Ted said, "We will pray for you and believe god will show you what to do". I kind of thought it was funny when Pastor Ted said this because his god isn't the same god this pastor preaches about.

Pastor Ted and I left and went back to his house because he wanted to show me my surprise; he went out and bought me a nice motor cycle, he said, "You will be 18 soon so this is just an early gift". I love to hear the roar of my bike because there's nothing like listening to a Harley. He let me know that Evil will be getting one of the group to teach me how to ride my new bike.

Pastor Ted drove me home and said, "We will get together tomorrow, ok?" I was all excited.

The next day I woke up and I smelt like a barbecue burning in my house but couldn't figure out where it was coming from, then the phone rang and Pastor Ted said that Pastor Mike came over this morning and that an angel appeared to him and said don't build your church because god has called you to quit the ministry because he's very disappointed in you, so just go back to driving a semi.

CHAPTER 5

My pastor then started giving me different assignments to do, to either deliver something or pick something up on my cool bike. Little by little I got really good on my bike.

One day I got stopped by a police officer in the next town over and when he began to question me, I told him I was picking up a package for my pastor, Pastor Ted, fear then came over this police officer and it was so shocking because I knew there was much more going on than what I was actually seeing because this police officer apologized to me several times and said just be careful.

It was so strange though because no matter where I went I always felt like a nervous energy because I knew someone or something was watching me but what? Who was interested in me?

I finally made it back to the pastor's home and he said, "Everything ok?" and I said, "Yes, but was wondering when can we go and see the family again and all those cool bikes?" But he said, "My young friend, they left because of another war that they decided to get into with another biker gang, but some day so many will be shocked that the war they fight is not at all with whom they think it is". I asked him, "What do you mean?" And he said, "Soon you will discover, just like that Pastor Mike blinded by ignorance, because of not understanding who the real battle is with".

Well then he said, "I need you to go to Black Mountain, there's a mechanic in that town called Spider, he had a letter mailed to several places that was mailed back to him with important information. it will take you about an hour to get there and an hour back, ok? I will take care of your lunch at the Snake Pit there in that town".

I then got on my bike and went home just real quick and my mom was home and she said, "Someone has put over $2 000 in my bank account but they refused to tell me who put it there, so I am able to catch up on several bills now. I don't know what is happening but finally for the first time in life I feel like I am going somewhere. As dumb as it sounds, ever since someone gave me this crystal at one of our bowling league parties it has a strange symbol in it but every time I take it off I feel something is wrong, so I keep it on me at all times. So how are you doing?" We talked a little bit and then I told her I needed to go and do something for the pastor.

So I took off to this next town over and I finally got there, it was a bigger town than I was expecting, but I finally made it to the garage where you could tell they were working on cars. This giant came out from inside of the garage, he was well over 6 feet tall, long black hair and had a horrible scar of a cut along the side of his face and he was very well built. Then he came over to me and I said, "Spider?" and he said, "Yes, let's go to the Snake Pit", so I jumped in his truck and we went to the restaurant. I said, "Busy day?" and he just said, "Not now, wait".

At first I felt scared but after we went to the restaurant I noticed he was a great guy to talk to. He handed me an envelope after lunch and said, "Don't let anyone see what's inside". I thought what could be so important in just a brown business size envelope you would use to mail a letter? Then he said, "Some will die and some will have to be sacrificed because of that letter but it is all for the glory of power". What was so strange is I never really felt so much evil as I did when my hand made contact with the letter so I just wanted to get it out of my pocket.

On the way back home I stopped at a gas station and I saw a black shadow come near me, well this terrified me so I just paid for my gasoline and left.

Finally I made it back home and went right away to the pastor's house and he was in his office so I went down there and gave it to him. I said, "What is so important about this letter? I don't understand". He said, "Young man, I am about ready to help you discover a world that most will never believe or accept it as being real, but I live by the concept of the beast and everyone around you is living by the beast as well. The question is, will you either bend your knee to the code of the beast or will you pretend that the beast isn't real so you get caught up doing this or that? But your destiny is fulfilled, either love the beast and do what he says or die like the fools desiring just a piece of bread, while those that worship the beast live in a nice home with all kinds of luxury".

Then my pastor took out a United States map and said, "Draw a line on this map of the cities I tell you", so I said ok. "San Antonio, TX, Little Rock, AR, Minneapolis, MN, Casper, WY, Albuquerque, NM, now look close what do you see?" I said, "I am not sure". He said," Don't you see it?" I said, "Oh, a pentagram", "Correct", he said. Then he said, "13 witches from each State channel their thoughts to one another and then 33 of the wealthiest men in those five states will have sex with the 13 most powerful witches of those states and 13 babies of wealthy people every year must die in those five states

But here's the key factor, as you draw your line anyone living in that pentagram design, living in a spider web, which means that if the beast says I want that woman or man they will have a hit on them. But here's the funny part, if the witch who called up the hit says I want them dead at 5:15 pm on Saturday, to fulfill the law we must make sure the person is dead as close to that time as possible, so if they are at a movie theater or on a plane, or even at school many innocent people will die just because they were around someone that has been called to be a sacrifice. I have seen so many innocent people die.

Then the 13 wealthiest men and the 13 wealthiest women will play some of the dumbest games and this will seal so many people's fate. Just imagine playing chess or checkers with people's lives, plus knowing that at times you have to use your own child or spouse as a sacrifice for the greater good of all mankind. See, so many think my destiny is about finding my place in a society that cares nothing about you. You are either in the game as a master calling the shots or you just a toy that could be destroyed at any time". So I asked him, "Are you one of the masters?" and he explained, "No my young friend, I help people understand where they belong".

He then explained, "See, these witches from all over will fly somewhere and it will appear as if they are going to a women's retreat or just on vacation. They are not allowed to talk to one another, in fact, so many spies are watching. They will then play a game the first night called, "Find the 13 items listed on the list", each witch from her district or state will pull a paper out of a pit bull's head on a platter and then you have to read the items out loud.

Some women are stupid enough to say that this is dumb to do, or this is a dumb list, but by voicing your opinion you now have sealed your fate because three black witches, who have spies, if you speak openly against them or the game your name will go in a black book, which most movies show it as being a place to keep track of ex-boyfriends or ex-girlfriends, but in reality it is a book that has names of those that speak against something. If your name gets put in the black book your fate is sealed and you will be eaten alive by an Anaconda snake. See, sometimes on the list will be really dumb things but too many forget the beast loves to humiliate people to see where their loyalty truly is.

I have personally seen people throw their grandchild in a fire, blow their wife's brains out with a 357 mag, or I have seen a woman two days before her wedding date one moment make out with her fiancé, then be kissing his throat and then without any warning slit his throat with a razor that was under her tongue. Also I have seen a person start up a race war right in a neighborhood just for the greater good. I have seen someone take pure heroin and give it to their best friend just because they were promised this or that.

See my dear young friend, when the F.B.I or A.T.F are not making any big busts lately they will find something to go after, so let me put it this way; instead of someone busting a child trafficking operation, they give the Feds over a 100 thousand dollars' worth of guns and over a million dollars' worth of drugs to seize. Then about three months later almost everybody has forgotten about it, so you pay someone some money and get your drugs and guns back. See; even if you don't get any of it back everyone will be soaking in their glory of the big bust that now it will be easier to transport even larger quantities into the United States. We even have people that will act like the big boss for a year, then when the F.B.I, I.C.E, or A.T.F move in and make the arrest they will offer that person's family a generous blessing to where most will get a house and the law will stay away from all their activities for 20 or 30 years.

So many have sold their soul without even knowing it because when you become indebted to these people it will never be paid in full so they can control every single thing in your life and they own everything that means something to you.

I knew a heroin addict that was going through living hell, just needing a fix and they put him in a room with the needle full of heroin with a foot over his head, that junkie went insane trying to get it, they tied cement blocks weighing over 200 ibs on each arm so he couldn't lift his arms so he went insane. Crying and begging for mercy. He had diarrhea and vomit all over him but they just watched him with a camera laughing and taking bets to see how long he would survive. But, like I said, he went insane and he lost his mind completely so they just fed him to my cousin's pit bulls. See, these people are very cruel but if you help them they will help you".

CHAPTER 6

W ell, my pastor shared something very deep with me that made sense, that where there is smoke there normally is fire but too many are too weak to understand this. I thought it was so bizarre. He pointed out to me that the closer you get to the beast the more you trust and want to taste his evil, but people who claim to love their God or love Jesus barely pray at all and their faith most of the time is so weak.

You can't really figure out who is a real Christian because so many who claim to love their God as soon as they get a taste of money, success, power and sexual enticements they fall away one by one claiming to the world that they still love God but down deep inside their hunger and lust is for the things of the beast, so hearing people sing and wanting the things of God is just almost a joke because as soon as they taste the things of the world they want more of the world.

My friend, one night a young man was praying and wondering what to do with his life and he said, "God, not my will but Your will", well right then and there a Demon who many worship and loved, which is called the Python Spirit, this spirit said to the young man, "Yes, you can do God's will but you will never be promised anything all that great and you will never truly have success or fame and you will just work a boring job trying to pay your bills. But if you sell your soul to me and serve the true beast I will promise to give you success and power like you could never imagine but if you decide to try to get rid of any one of my spirit friends out of your life I will make your children suffer greatly and you will watch".

Well this man is one of the most powerful, well-known presidents and wealthiest men to ever live, in fact, when they buried him he was put in a gold engraved coffin, yes he was that wealthy.

See, my young friend, they are watching you; when you masturbated they were there watching, when you were feeling like someone was choking you, Python had her tongue around you in the spirit. See, spirits are watching you all the time and planting new ideas in your mind. Do you see why so many are coming up with this or that conspiracy thinking that the government is doing this or that to them? How stupid and silly can you get? So many don't realize the beast is blinding them so they will do his will but they don't reap any benefits for it.

See, it's like this; one gang will war with another gang, killing and raping, for what? A little bit of money and property, so they are doing the beast a favor, doing his evil deeds for him. But what if these people were to stop thinking so small and they wanted to help control a whole entire city or state using the same force, but now they are making money and getting power handed to them daily while they sit back in a leather chair playing chess, watching nude chicks get beheaded or watching someone put a bullet into someone, all out of just having fun with plenty of food.

Women especially go to church to get involved in a prayer group, start spreading gossip, claiming it's all ok because their heart was in the right place, see, if they would just offer their lives over to the beast their gossip would be rewarded. So many do evil things claiming their heart was in the right place, or claiming that they felt right about it, or claiming God told them to do it, lies upon lies. Just admit that you have turned your will and life over to the beast that's why you did what you did. When a pastor falls into a sexual relationship with another woman or man it almost makes you laugh because of all the excuses they use.

"Why do you think, young man, Bigfoot or UFOs are so popular but yet there is very little proof? If you are a deer hunter you look for the droppings of a deer or if you are a bear hunter you will see bear droppings but nobody yet has found any crap of a Bigfoot because as long as the beast can distract people from seeing the truth he will blind you.

So many know that where there is smoke there most of the time is a fire but most don't want to open that door of truth, so instead of putting out the fire they only put water on the door to life, not ever putting out the fire on the other side because they are gutless and fearful of the truth. Instead of waging a war against the beast most try to act cool or so powerful by coming against drug lords or those who are cult leaders. If you want to destroy the sheep destroy its master. Evil is all around you and everyone else but the question is will you become friends with it or allow it to destroy you? The choice is yours".

I never realized that what my pastor was saying would be so true, these spirit beings are wanting to come inside me and help guide me to a greater life, but the question is, I never could get a straight answer, what is the cost because I just know everything comes with a cost, right, or am I wrong?

Well later that day the pastor called me at home after I left and said, "Are you ok? I dont want to scare you but when you connect with your spirit guide you can't imagine the doors that could open for you".

Well I wanted to be alone for a while so I left a note for my mom and I went on a long bike ride and went to the restaurant, the Snake Pit, while I was there I saw a person come in dressed up really nicely and they were meeting someone also dressed up nicely. As I was listening to their conversation, these men were talking about how we need a better president and better laws and I just wanted to laugh because so many are blind to what is going on. Wars are happening all over, gangs fighting for more areas, serial killers wanting someone to know they're out there killing, so many are worshiping this and that god and now so many claim Allah or Mohammed are full of truth. But then Mega racist groups claim that the grand dragon is truth. But then Mormons claim there is only truth in their prophet, while Jehovah Witnesses claim they are the only way, but does anyone know the truth?

Then to my complete surprise Spider walked in with Evil, these are both men I like and admire, they saw me and said, "How are you, little man?" And I said, "Ok but just trying to figure things out" and Spider said, "Don't try, just be led".

Then Spider said something I have never heard of before, "Do what thou wilt shall be the whole of the law". When he said this it was like an incredible power was speaking at the same time he was speaking. So I asked him what does it mean and he said, "Do what you want to do, don't put any trust in any "so called" faith, Holy Bible or what a pastor says, do what you want to and just live by that code. See the code of the law to live by is, If it feels good, sounds good, tastes good, pleases you, makes you feel good, or it brings deep pleasure to you how can it be wrong?"

Then Spider said, "You should just become one of us, no more wondering just come with us and we will teach you a new way and it will shock you but you will be a new person and you will gain the deep desires you want".

CHAPTER 7

That night I went to a secret meeting; they met deep in the woods somewhere, I could tell because I could hear the truck driving over branches and going through mud, I was blindfolded but then they put a mask on me but I saw through the mask.

I was in a cave, all my clothes were taken off of me and I felt fear in a way that I have never felt fear before. Then I saw this creature that looked just like a hairy monster stand before me and he touched me sexually, then I could feel him go inside of me and I knew then that something was very wrong but I felt as if I was someone new.

Then I saw I was standing on a huge board with strange markings and all of a sudden I looked and realized that men and women with only masks on their faces were in the nude also standing on this board and I heard a voice say, "Yes, you are all standing on an Ouija board, get prepared, your new birth is about to take place". Then I felt something be put up my anus and I felt as if I was having sex with a slimy snake, as if a snake with claws was pulling on me while licking me all over. It felt good but I thought this is wrong I am enjoying having sex with an animal.

Then I saw this guy in front of me masturbate in a bowl. Then I saw another person pee in the bowl. Then this woman walked up and slit her wrist and I watched all that blood go in the bowl. Then another person took a crap in front of me and it all went in the bowl, then I saw a Billy goat and a baby lamb have their throat slit in front of me and their blood went in the bowl.

Then this guy that looked just like a witchdoctor that you would see in a magazine, came up to the bowl and was dancing and singing to it and he then slit a chicken's throat and all of its blood went in the bowl. Then a bathtub was brought in and a huge bull was lifted up and they put this bull in the bathtub and then they slit its throat.

Then all around me people began to chant and scream, "The beast lives". Then I looked around and candles were lit and then I realized I am in a pentagram. Then as all the blood was filling the tub I heard, "Now children of the beast, drink the power of the anointing of power, wealth and take it all in but if you dare waste a drop you shall surly die". Then I heard, "All my new children, drink from the bowl but if you dare puke or spill it your blood will be one with the bulls".

Well I knew I had to drink it, so they went down the line and this woman puked so I knew she was going to suffer, but what they did was so cruel, they tied her to a post and hooked her breast up to an electrical charge, then they put a snake up in her, tied her hands and feet and then turned the electricity on. She was screaming with such a wicked scream because she was claiming the snake was biting her inside.

Then they smeared some type of lotion on her breast and they put these bizarre worms all over her breast and they were eating her skin and going inside of her. Then they put a bunch in her mouth and they were crawling down her throat. The whole time she was begging to die but not one person could care because they began to chant and then all of a sudden I heard spirits say, "Enter the child and say if you want more of us, just ask", so I said, "Yes", and at least 15 spirits came inside of me. Then I was given a drink and I passed out and the next day I woke up in my bed.

After waking up I realized I wasn't all alone anymore, I literally had other voices speaking to me all from within. I was so shocked that so many voices were speaking at one time, I realized I would go insane or do something bizarre if I didn't learn how to control this.

The pastor called me, Pastor Ted that is my dear friend, he said, "Wasn't last night incredible?" I wasn't sure what to say because I knew I wasn't the same and now I am seeing things, I wanted to find out if any of this was true or am I just imaging stuff. I told my pastor, "I gotta go"

I got cleaned up and jumped on my bike and headed North, opposite from the direction of the Snake Pit, I road easily for about two hours and came to this place called Valley Peaks, I don't know what I was in search of but I saw a sign that said, "Do you want to be free from guilt and sin?" So I went to it and I saw this guy cleaning garbage outside, so I said, "Hello, I was wondering if the pastor was in?"

He said, "Hello, I am Pastor John, how can I help you?" I let him know that I see shadows move and hear voices at times, I have a lot of severe nightmares and I think I have spirits living in me. This pastor shocked me he said, "Since the apostles died out we have no need for the power of God to be preached anymore, just ask Jesus to come inside you and your life will be so much better". I said "I have met people who love God a lot but they are poor and they struggle, so I don't understand"

He said, "If you believe Satan has no power then life becomes easy, these people you talk about live in defeat because spirits are no longer on the earth now, so they probably need professional help". I asked one more question, "Do you believe in Devil worshipers?" and he laughed and he said, "That is silly, that is like believing in Superman". I was so shocked because just last night I know what I was watching and they were worshiping evil.

Well I got on my bike and headed back. Then I saw this really nice church and it said, "All are welcome", so I went in and the secretary said, "Hi, how can I help you?" I said, "Can I see a pastor or just talk to one?" She said, "Well let me see most of them are only by appointment."

So I waited and this man came out and said, "Hello, I am Pastor Tom, let's go to my office and chat". I asked him, "Do you believe that a person can see shadows move or hear voices, or even feel depressed at times for no reason?" He looked at me and said, "Well, young man, if someone comes to me and starts talking about the devil or experiencing strange things I highly recommend that they go and see a professional because, see, we are called to live a happy and peaceful life and we don't need to focus on any evil things".

I went back home and thought, ok this is just silly, and none of this is real so I just decided that all of it was phony.

I made it home and I crashed out on the couch and I heard a voice after a while, so I thought my mom is home and the TV is on, so I just buried my head under the pillow and went back to sleep.

After a while I thought I should wake up and I looked straight ahead staring at the chair in the living room and I heard it as clear as day, "My child, sell your soul to me, yes sell your soul and just tell me what you want and it is yours". I then looked in the corner and to my shock the beings were there just talking and the TV was off. I was so scared, not knowing what to do, then I heard it again, "Sell your soul", then I jumped up and they were all gone and there was silence in the house. I started to cry because I realized this was all real but if it wasn't did I lose my mind? I heard what those pastors said but what if they were so blind that they can't see anything in the paranormal?

I decided I need to go out and I found a small keg going on just a couple of blocks away from my house, so I went in and introduced myself.

CHAPTER 8

I met this girl named Nikki, she and I became instant friends, she was explaining how she was clairvoyance and how she can listen and spirits will tell her things. So I asked her, "Do you see things?" She said, "Yes but I feel things as well." I didn't really want to leave but since it was getting late I had to leave, so I did.

I lay there in bed thinking about Nikki, wondering what she was doing, then I felt a warm hand touch my cheek and at first it scared me but then I knew I just knew it was Nikki.

Well the next day I woke up and I knew someone was watching me and when I opened my eyes Nikki was sitting there, I said, "What are you doing?" She said, "I am chanting over your clothes, they will speak to me so no matter how apart we ever are they will tell me how you are doing."

I got up and took a shower and I said, "You have to meet my pastor he is so great", so we went to see Pastor Ted, I introduced them and came to find out that they already knew each other.

Nikki was the granddaughter to one of the most powerful black witches in the state. My pastor said, "You are going to be well taken care of by this young woman". Then he said, "Nikki, have him meet your mom and grandmother". Nikki said, "Yes the cards will speak" and my pastor said, "Nikki, you are so correct the cards will speak loudly" but I had no idea, so I said, "What are you all talking about?" Nikki then looked at me with those beautiful darkened eyes and said, "Tarot cards, my grandmother is an expert at it and she has helped attorneys, doctors, business owners and several other become wealthy".

My pastor then said, "My young friend I have to be flying to Seattle Washington tomorrow, several witches are asking me to take a vacation so I need to see what is going on". I said, "Wow, so you are going to fly from Butte Montana to Seattle, Washington?" He just smiled and said, "Never, I will go to a place called Sand Point, Idaho then to a city called Spokane and then off to Seattle. See my young friend, Seattle has so many powerful witches there and so many are getting deeper into their powers. On the way there I have to stop by and say, hi". I gave him a hug and said goodbye.

That afternoon Nikki and I went for a bike ride, it was so much fun just getting out and meeting people.

Later that night we went to a keg and the people there were playing with an Ouija board. Nikki said to some people, "Don't laugh at the board you are offending the spirits and causing them to be aroused", they just laughed at her. I felt a presence come into the living room where they were playing with the Ouija board and all of a sudden Nikki became filled with anger and suddenly I could slice the fear in the room with a knife, it was that thick. Then all of a sudden the table began to shake and people began to freak out, yelling and screaming, running all over but the lamp fell over so you could barely see except for the kitchen light. Well, the guy making fun of the board was stepped on and his neck was snapped.

We didn't know what to do so they called the sheriff and he came and got the body, I was in shock and so was Nikki, so Nikki just ended up staying with me all night sleeping on my couch with me.

The next day I was still really bothered about all of this and so was Nikki, so we went to the house where the keg was to see what was happening and to our surprise the sheriff was there, he saw us so we stopped to talk to him and he said, "Oh, your friend is fine we took him home this morning". He then said to one of the deputies, "He was hated here so we took him to the edge of town with a suitcase and we left him there. It was odd but young people can never make up their mind at times".

The Sheriff then just left. I looked at Nikki and then she stared right in my eyes and we both knew that guy was dead. I am so shocked because why cover this up and what did they do with his body? Who would want a dead body?

Nikki and I decided that we needed answers so our journey began to find out why a dead person was no longer to be found.

That afternoon we decided to see if anyone at the keg had any answers but everyone just looked at us as if we had lost our minds, everyone said, "You are joking, the guy's name was Bryan and he wasn't dead so let it go".

Whilst we were there this girl came out and said, "Nikki, I know you, your mother is my mom's aunts best friend". Nikki then said, "Oh wow, Tracy it's you." She said, "Yes". She said Bryan was dead and I know it but you don't realize what you are getting into.

Tracy said, "There's this Warlock that is friends with some of the most powerful people you could meet, he just moved his whole entire empire that he ran, he now owns three gentlemen's clubs, one liquor store and now he has just bought that convenient store west of town with that small gas station. Be careful of him he is well known for having people disappear and he is well known throughout Seattle as a trafficker. He kidnaps children and adults and uses them as sex slaves all over.

Be very careful both of you. I don't know if you ever heard of the secret code, the razor, but I will warn you don't ever mention that around anyone ever".

So I asked what is it, Tracy said, "They traumatize you to the point where you crack, they use a certain word and now you are a human soldier to the point where you have no memory of it at all. Yes, they are actually making human soldiers all for the sake of the new world order to where these people have super strength, thinking they are living normal lives but no, they are actually normal till they hear the code word then they become super soldiers with no consciences, it sounds bizarre but it's true. So many are like they have no heart at all, it's like they are so consumed in evil by making men and women be like this".

Well, as Nikki and I started to ask questions it became strange, so we headed to the Snake Pit to see if Spider was there, he was and he came out to see us and we told him about what went on but he pointed out that we are way over our heads because a dead body can be used to transport drugs because they will gut it out, put two or three kilos of cocaine in the stomach area then sew it up, then clean it up. Or you can use a dead body to manipulate people by using fear tactics so they back off because a super, very powerful group of men are making an elite group to destroy anyone that doesn't want to worship the beast.

I felt like we were reading a comic book. But as time went on I started to understand that the Holy Bible had a lot of powerful secrets of what was going to happen but the one who wins this war isn't correct but the war is so true.

I told Nikki we need to leave so we left. But it amazed me how so many don't see why things are happening when it is spelt out plain and simple. I then began to explain to Nikki that this is all part of the great dragon coming to power, but even she said to me, "How can anyone trust anything written years ago?"

So I had to figure out what the razor meant and who was behind it. There are just so many secrets to what is going on but it seems only a few know about this or that part so I had to get answers.

CHAPTER 9

Well we left that area and went back home. I checked the pastor's mail for him and there was an envelope that wasn't sealed very well and it said, "Don't share; the Razor is coming", so I told Nikki and she said can I see it?" And she tilted it sideways and the letter fell out, she picked it up and it said, "UFOs are coming get ready!" Well it seemed like so many things were happening that it was impossible to keep track of what was really happening.

Then I realized that it was the book of codes that I saw in the pastor's house, so I knew it would be ok to take it off the book shelf. As I began to read it, it all began to make sense because so many alarms were going off in my head and so many things were happening so quickly that I realized that there was a major war going on and nobody could see it because everyone was being distracted with this or that.

It was like people were like frogs being put in water to where the temperature was rising but nobody saw that all the frogs were being cooked to death but now humans are in the pan but nobody wants to admit to truth and all these "so called" conspiracy theories are just make matters worse because while they are attacking a small fire a major fire is burning but they can't see it because they are being blinded. But who is behind all of this and why?

I told Nikki what I am seeing happening but she wasn't interested. So I began to really wonder what is the truth? I was watching the news as Nikki was taking an afternoon nap and the news reporter was reporting things happening in the United States, but why isn't anyone seeing simple truths?

The next couple of days Nikki and I were just hanging out and just having fun and we put on a barbecue for our friends and the pastor called me finally, I said, "Pastor Ted how is Seattle?" And he was explaining it was awesome but several witches want to make that area their home, so get ready because so many homes will be going up and at night covens will start praying over the area. I then told him about the code razor I had gotten information on, he said, "You are very bright young man, but now things are getting very intense, 13 of the most powerful witches from the United States will be coming there and praying, as well as the 13 most powerful leaders who are deeply devoted to Lucifer are also coming to pray there, and 13 of the most powerful and wealthy world leaders will be there as well. I realized now if all these world leaders are coming in what is happening?

I decided to go for a walk while Nikki was cooking dinner and my spirit guide said, "Prepare the way for the beast is coming". And I asked what does this mean and my spirit guide said, "Every aspect of life, the new world order is a group of men who have sold their souls to the beast to where they could have all their sexual, perverted, lust, power and desires fulfilled. Every aspect of life has been taken over so no one will see that the coming hour of our king and lord is about to come to pass.

It is funny, instead of people being concerned about their freedom; people are being blinded with lingerie advertisements, sexual sitcoms, comedies that mock God in every way. The world that God created and He is so proud of has turned its back on Him to where people are more interested in a good bottle of wine or a sleazy movie more than they are interested in what a "so called" preacher has to say. Look, my friend, even pastors are becoming so weak minded, they either want to take their life or they preach all about money and prosperity.

You see my friend, there are six things that the beast is taking away to where preachers won't talk about them and they are considered outlaw words that are just pointless to the point that these words will not even be spoken or preached about anymore, that is the Cross, the Blood, Jesus Christ's name, resurrection, claiming that it should be God's will not our will. See, these things will even be removed from all religious writings because Jesus has caused wars and the cross is very offensive. The word sin is just wrong, how dare some one judge you because you find an animal sexually attractive?

See, the church has become so judgmental and so wrong, so many are not getting it, the beast offers love, feeling good, happiness, pleasure and feeling good about yourself. The bible is just so judgmental and so wrong.

I went back and my spirit guide wanted to share more about all of this and it all sounds great but I am wondering deep down inside what's the point to all of this?

Well as time went by I began to think about suicide daily and I wondered should I just kill everyone and that way none of this evil would grow anymore but who is really in control?

After several months my dad is coming home, he has been gone so long fighting in a war because when your dad is a Marine you get called and ordered to make peace for a country that doesn't want you there. Well in some ways I feel like I should be excited but he hasn't ever thought much of me and when he found out I can't go in the Corps he hasn't thought much of me. My mother likes me at times but I feel like she just wants me to go out on my own and just drift somewhere else.

It is interesting knowing that ever since I was just a very young person I have often thought why am I alive? What's the point to all this and why can't people just love or accept me just the way I am? Over and over again I wasn't smart enough to do this or that or good enough, I was looked down on because I was small, or not mechanically inclined. It didn't matter what I did it was never good enough. Well as time went on I realized there was no point to life so I attempted suicide, but what happened? How could I live through this?

CHAPTER 10

W ell one day Nikki said to me, "I want you to meet my grandmother", so we went to go and visit her. The house was covered in thorn bushes growing up all around it, in fact, it looked like
just one of those horror story movie houses, the paint was coming
off and there were two bizarre old statues of these lions with wings
in front of them but they are very evil looking with big teeth.

I went inside and immediately I felt something like a snake
slither over my groin and it was sexually touching me. I felt very
paranoid being in there. Then I heard what sounded like a baby
crying, but why I thought?

Nikki said, "Do you want to see the house?" So I said, "Sure."
Well as we walked throughout the house I noticed that one room
was boarded up and I said, "Why is this room boarded up?" And
she said, "My grandmother had a son but one night during a ritual
her son choked to death so they made an alter for the little one but
my grandmother told everyone that this room needs to be boarded
up because I want the little one to come back at any time and be at
peace".

So Nikki said, "Every now and then you will hear a baby playing
in that room and if you climb up on a ladder and look in the window
you will see where the toys and clothes are and then the next day
they are moved but nobody can go in there".

Then as we walked around I literally saw a shadow of like a man walking and I said, "Who was that?" Nikki started to giggle and she said, "That was my grandfather, he died about three years ago so my grandmother had so many witches here summoning up spirits to get her husband to stay here that now his spirit just roams around the house". I said, "Well Nikki, I need you to know that when we first came in I felt like someone sexually touched me", she said, "You are so funny, the eyes and walls are alive, can't you feel it?" The blood of victims was used to mix with the paint to paint this house, isn't that funny?"

Well her grandmother called us and said, "Young man, the cards are telling me that you know the truth, you see and hear what is the truth". Then she said, "Walk with the beast and you will have everything you could ever imagine". I wanted to go so I said, "That is wonderful, thank you". Then she grabbed my hand and gave me a bizarre kiss for her being a grandmother, she put her tongue in my mouth and said, "I taste the sweetness in you". So being shocked I just said, "Ok", then I said, "Nikki are you ready?" And so we left.

As we were going down the road Nikki shocked me, she said, "After grandfather died I felt so bad for my grandmother so I put down a tarp on my grandfather's office floor and got on my knees in the nude and then I cut my wrist and hands, then I raised them up towards the ceiling and watched the blood drip down on my face and then it dripped all over my breast and then it just went down my stomach, it was so beautiful looking, I just couldn't stop watching it in the mirror and then two hands came out of the mirror and started touching me sexually, so I just said, "I am yours, be one with me".

All of a sudden I could see and hear things that were incredible. I actually saw two girls at school speaking against me while they were in in the girls' locker room while I was in the parking lot, so I said to the spirits, "If you cause these girls to be in a severe car accident after school I will offer myself sexually to you".

Well, two days later a logging truck had its chain snap while on the road next to them and as the chain snapped it was like an incredible whip that hit the windshield with so much force it went right through the window and cut off the leg of one of the girls, then one of the side bars crashed on the car so both were pinned down and then the logs came crashing down on the car but they were slowly being crushed little by little.

Eye witnesses said they could both just hear screaming and crying. But about every two minutes the logs would move and just smash the car even more. Over 45 people just watched their car be flattened just like a pancake, knowing two teen girls were inside. Then blood was going all over and it was like every time the logs shifted it was like someone popped a balloon. Then as this big tow truck was coming down the road the logs shifted one more time and the car went flat and the screaming and yelling stopped. That night I was laughing till I fell asleep".

Then I was raped and forced to have sex with so many spirits that I knew I was in way over my head. I was bitten well over a hundred times, I was choked, slugged and I knew things were being shoved in my anus, plus my insides felt like they were being ripped out. The suffering didn't stop till the sunlight came through the window the next morning. I learnt a very powerful lesson. But I did know one thing, black magic isn't just something to talk about it is real.

We then went to go and get something to eat and I just wanted something easy and fast so we went to a burger place. It was just bizarre, this woman walked up to us as we were waiting in line and said, "You are into evil, I see it. You are going to Hell there's no hope for you". I was shocked because this has never happened before, I never saw myself as a bad person; just lost, wanting to be loved and accepted by someone. The woman just kept telling Nikki and me how we are on our way to Hell.

We left and went to a taco place. Three people moved out of our way and we were wondering what was going on, everyone acts so scared of us. Nikki said, "This is creepy", so I just said, "Let's just order and then go".

Then as we were waiting to order I saw the reflection of me on this banner they had hanging on the front counter side wall, I literally saw like a monster on my shoulder, so I said to Nikki, "Order for me, I have to use the bathroom".

I went in the bathroom and I looked in the mirror and as clear as day there was a very evil and wicked looking thing stuck to me and it was saying evil things, so I said, "Leave me!" but it threw me into the counter, my back went backwards as if I was trying to grab my feet backwards while standing up, I was floored and in shock. I couldn't believe I was able to do this, then this spirit said as clear as day, "If you think that was cool that is nothing compared to what you can do with us living in you".

Then as soon as I was done being freaked out I went out to join Nikki and I told her what I saw, she said, "Well of course, but you are not supposed to see him, you only feel him". Then she said, "I know what's going on", yes, people are most likely feeling the evil around you now because the spirits in you are more powerful than the spirits in me, but my spirits I have an awesome relationship with, but you are just getting to know them".

She then said, "Didn't you notice I can pull things out of a hot oven but never wear mittens? Or I have learnt that I can touch someone sexually just because I am having an out of the body experience even if it's a thousand miles away because there's no distance in the paranormal. Or the coolest thing that I love is astro-projection. See my dear loving boyfriend, quit resisting them and just give yourself over to these spirits in you because they want to help you and not hurt you".

Well Nikki and I got our food and she showed me how to do something right there after we sat down. She said, "See that big guy over there?" I said, "Yes", she then said, "Watch him", so I did and she said, "Spirits of fear I summon you and I am asking you to make that guy become so nervous he will forget to chew up his food and then he will swallow and choke". Well I saw it with my own eyes.

Then we left after eating. We got on the bike and at a four way stop Nikki said, "Spirits of confusion and distraction I summon you to cause two people to become lost in their thoughts and cause an accident right away". We then went into a parking lot and within just five minutes two people ran the stop sign and crashed their cars and one of them was an elderly man. And then we saw a police car and an E.M.T car show up and they got out a body bag because the elderly man died.

Nikki was so proud of herself because she said, "Did you feel that?" I said, "What?" She said, "The beast, our father, invited him in so he will live in such a cool place. Right under our feet is Hell and they get all the drugs, alcohol, sex, rock music and partying they want. Plus in Hell you can sleep in and do what you want. Heaven looks so boring and to know that you will sit around just worshiping God all day, but no sex and no partying I can't imagine.

Well then we went to a playground and Nikki was cursing so many children and one by one these children were falling and getting hurt or they were being thrown off of this or that. Well finally I said, "Let's go back and just play some games on the computer for a while, ok." So we headed back to my house. But all the way there I literally heard "You are a worthless person, just take your life, Nikki doesn't want you, you are just a very dumb person.

We then arrived back at my house.

Well as time went on it seems like the tormenting just gets worse, I had visions of taking my own life. At times I get so depressed I would just daydream about who would come to my funeral and who would really be bothered about me? Day and night I would daydream about how I was going to kill myself but at times I would stop myself and wonder what was the point to this "so called" life? I have hated most of my life and, in fact, I am surprised that I haven't taken my life yet.

Nikki mentioned to me that she felt that life was pointless and it had no meaning, so I guess I didn't see the clues because I felt God or whoever made me must have wasted His time making a creation that just rejected and hated Him.

CHAPTER 11

One night Nikki asked me if I would hold her forever and I said, "Yes", so she said, "Let's die together tonight and make it romantic". So she cooked us a nice dinner and then she put a whole bunch of pills of different things in a soda can and we shared it. Then as we sat there on the couch holding each other I fell asleep.

Then I woke up and ran to the bathroom and started to vomit. Then I thought what about Nikki, so I ran to check on her but she died. There was nothing that I could do and I wasn't going to let them put her in the ground, so I picked up her little body and put her in my bed in my room.

As I lay there holding her I began to feel a strong sense that I should make love to her but I thought wouldn't that be inhuman? Is this not evil to think this way? Then I thought she might think so but she is dead so why would she care?

Well I got up and started to comb her hair and then I just held her in my arms crying so I kissed her. Then I found myself looking down her shirt, so I knew right then and there I had to make love to her. So I undressed her and started making love to her, her little body just flopped as if she was a piece of steak on a barbecue. It was a magical moment and I felt that what I was doing is very evil, but on the other hand it was magical because I wanted to be close to her, but when they bury her it is over, there she will just lie in the dirt.

Well after I got done getting off I just lay there being inside of her, she was so cold and felt so stiff. When I put my tongue in her mouth, I didn't know that it would be so dry inside in her mouth, as if my tongue was on a cardboard box. I then got up and got dressed and then I dressed her. I thought I should call someone to say she had died, so I just put my sweats on her and then I put the covers over her where she lay so peacefully in my bed. All I could do was cry and beg that she would come back to me.

Well, Pastor Ted called me and said, "Hey, we must get together, I miss chatting with you". As I was sitting there talking to him I looked through the corner of my eye at my large mirror and I literally saw Nikki sit up and look at me, I was so terrified that I hung up on the pastor. I ran over to the bed and Nikki was covered up, so I just said, "Oh good it was just my imagination". I then called the pastor back and apologized and he said, "No problem, so what happened?" I said, "Sorry, I saw something but it wasn't real".

Well that night my mom came home and we had dinner with my dad and then they said that they were we going out for a while, ok, have fun.

Well I knew that Nikki was going to start smelling so I had to take her somewhere but as I looked at her in my sweats she looked so good. I don't know why but the idea of having her masturbate me just turned me on, so I put a lot of oil on her hand and then I took my hand and put it over her hand and started masturbating with her hand. It was so magical and wonderful, then just as I came I saw Nikki turn her head and said, "Do you like it Rick?" I was so shocked to hear my own name, nobody ever called me by my own name, and this is impossible, I can't hear a dead person speak, so I dropped to my knees and realized I am insane. What is reality? Does it exist? I was so terrified that nothing made sense.

Well, according to the psychiatric ward, my dad heard me screaming and then realized there was a dead girl in my bed so they came and got me and I was put into a mental institution. The doctor came in and said, "You are not under arrest but you are awarded to the State because we feel you could be a danger to yourself. The young woman in your bed choked to death on her own vomit, because after examining her dead body she was too wiped out to lift her head so she chocked to death. I am very sorry. So can you tell me about how this dead woman ended up in your bed and why your sperm was found inside of her and all over her hand?" As the doctor began to ask questions I fell asleep.

I woke up and I felt like I was asleep for a very long time, so I asked the nurse checking my vitals what the date was and I found out that I was asleep or dozing in and out for over a month.

I finally was well enough to have a doctor speak to me, so the doctor was paged and he came and talked to me. He said to me, "My young friend, I am so sorry your girlfriend took her life. I hope you understand by wanting to have sex with her is normal but that won't bring her back. Well you are fine but I want you to see a licensed psychologist, I feel that this is what you need so I am going to release you but please understand you need help". Well he then said, "I feel you are safe to just let go but I want to make sure that you stay in this facility for at least 90 days, so just feel free to roam around and watch TV ok."

Well I couldn't believe it, I had to stay in this place all because of money; if you release a person before 90 days the insurance can then question you so I was just a pawn in a money scam. Everyone knows that when it's a paranormal problem you need to go through some sort of deliverance unless you want to be high and not function at all anymore as a person because they just keep you drugged up.

CHAPTER 12

Well finally I got to go home and I was so excited to see my stuff. A police car drove me home and my mom was so upset at me, claiming that I embarrassed her and my dad because I had sex with a dead girl. She felt I was not even human anymore. My dad, even though he doesn't like me said, "Son, if we can get you a good job you will be fine, you just need to make money".

My parents then left, so my pastor came over and said, "You don't realize it but, my young friend, you have no idea just how valuable you are to the beast or me. See, because you have gone off the deep end and you were committed now nobody will believe you, so now I want to teach you so much more because "so called" professionals are just too stupid to realize that so much evil is happening right under their noses but they can't see it because they refuse to believe it's real".

I was so happy that at least one person was happy to see me.

Well my pastor said, "Remember I told you that my office has a bunch of racism stuff in it but that is just a smoke screen to the truth. See, if people think I am into racism they say ok, but if I point out to them that the Swastika is a satanic symbol and I am deep into worshiping demons I would be locked up for a very long time. See, my friend, you can claim to worship Allah and they claim its freedom of religion. But if you worship a spirit or a demon they claim you are insane. What so many don't realize is that you look and see which has more power, and you find out that those who worship the beast, Lucifer, or a demon all have more power than anything near it.

Here is what I found interesting, "When I was 17 years old my mom was making me go to church and they always talked about how great God was and how awesome Jesus was but when a friend of mine came to church with me one time and he was wearing this T-shirt with a pentagram you should have seen it; everyone, even the pastor was so fearful and nobody even greeted him, so I knew in my heart who was the great and mighty god, it wasn't that God that they preach from the bible, it was the god who they call the beast or Lucifer. So I took all my stuff I had about Jesus and all my notes on bible studies and burned it all.

Then about a week later, it was snowing outside and was very cold outside, a Demon by the name of Raw stood before me said, "Do you want to see awesome power? Go outside in the freezing cold with no shirt or shoes or socks on, yes just bare feet and I will keep you warm, but if you see that the cold doesn't affect you I want you to invite me inside, deal? Ok?"

Well, all of my life I have never heard of a demon talking to a person and all of my life I have heard of a person asking Jesus to come in and live inside of them, but to invite a demon to come in and live? Well I thought the contest was silly and easy to win. So I put on just a pair of shorts and I had nothing else on, just shorts, no shoes, no socks and no shirt. I went outside and I was really hot and I saw like a ring of fire around me and this angel looking like being said, "What do you want, just tell me, I am wanting to help you get all your desires met?"

So I said, "Ok, I want a house, a big truck and to be able to travel and have plenty of money". So he said, "Invite me in as your lord". Well I did so and my life changed in a split second, I knew I had so much power living in me. I said, "Wow, I love this" And all of a sudden about 500 of these demonic looking like creatures were crawling all over me and around me saying, "Glory to the true living king, may the beast live forever".

Then later that day my mom got a call and she said, "Your granddad died and because you were his favorite grandson he left you his house and wealth". I was so crushed at the funeral, I couldn't stop crying and then Raw stood before me and said, "Swallow your tears and harden your heart it's time to claim war against the stupid saints who are trying to stop my kingdom from growing".

"Then I went to my grandfather's house which was mine now and I knew that there was something living there that I felt scared of, so I decided to just watch TV for a while but then the phone rang, so I got up to answer it and to my shock I saw this snake like being crawl through the wall and just slither into the kitchen and then into me, while I was on the phone listening to a stupid salesman, so I hung up and just stood there in awe. I don't know why but I peed all over the floor out of fear".

Well, I cleaned myself up and then I lay there on my grandfather's bed knowing this is my home, then I heard, "Don't fear us we just want to have sex with you", so all of a sudden I felt three claws on both sides of me holding me but it was like I was having sex with a woman but its body felt like slimy and had a body like an alligator. I felt so much force holding me that I thought I was going to die but then when I came it let me go. After that experience I don't know why but I felt the need for more sexual experiences.

I went into the basement of my grandfather's house and when I saw pentagrams on posters and codes written out with their meaning and saw how this was so well organized I knew I wanted this so I sold more and more of myself over to the beast to where I knew he lived in me. At that point I knew I was totally against everything I was raised with. See its odd, but I hear you talk about wanting to be loved and accepted but I also was never loved or accepted".

That was the first time my dear friend Pastor Ted shared his heart with me. Then he said, "My young friend, everything in life you do has a price tag on it, so many want to be wealthy so they learn to give up those that are so deep inside of their hearts but I have also met others that could have had it all but they were more interested in family than success. See, so many wanted success in Hollywood and in the music industry that they made their own signed contracts with the beast but nobody wants to admit it, but there's so many that the number would shock both of us.

But then there's those also who were never given any credit but always wanted to be a big football star or someone great but because they never made it they also signed their own contract with the beast asking for a group to listen to them and support their ideas.

Then you also have the "so called" money hungry pastor who denies the fact of how they became so successful but it's not hard just listen to their teachings, it's so crystal clear. A spirit said if you don't preach on sin, the cross, the power of God, praying in the spirit or repentance I will offer you great success. See, my young friend, so many have sold out to please the beast because he is the true awesome god of this world and he wants to help you find success".

I then started to figure this all out, that there was no hope for me and there was nothing in real life called love, it was just a myth. So many don't realize I just want to die but I have been called to live a life of deep sadness because why doesn't anyone just realize I just want someone that will love me and accept me for who I am with no strings attached?

It's odd that my Pastor Ted feels the same as I feel but he can't see past his own pain and sadness. If Pastor Ted had so much that he asked for why did he sound so hopeless and sad? I just couldn't stop thinking about this.

Well I decided that I needed something, but what? Feeling trapped in a life I don't want or even asked for, so what's the point? So I will take my life. So once again I was on a journey trying to figure out how can I take my life.

Well, I took a bunch of pills thinking this is it, I am done. But then the next day I woke up thinking why am I not wanted and nobody sees any value in me so why can't I just die? Why am I still alive?

CHAPTER 13

I got a call from Pastor Ted and he said, "There's a huge shipment of cocaine that has come in and I need to make sure that it goes to the right people but I am being handed the new codes for the witches and warlocks to come together with several mediums and psychics to pray as they channel their new ideas and thoughts into men and women that will be senators and sit on congress staff".

I said, "What?" And my pastor said, "Yes, they pray for leaders six years in advance. They know who will be their vice president six years in advance and their President several years ahead. See, there's a book they call "The Book of the Law", it is like a satanic calendar to where certain people who want to hold an office anywhere for any State or even the government must be willing to give up this or that. Nobody becomes successful till the Book of the Law says so".

See, ask yourself this my friend, "Why is it that when "so called" Christians put on prayer seminars they get all excited if two hundred show up, to when those that plan on exalting and sacrificing to Lucifer expect nothing less than five thousand plus worldwide?. People are channeling because they want that flow to come in them. So many, my young friend, were just like my pastor I had when I was young, they are weak and cowards, they speak so powerfully but they are just a waste of human breath. I will be so glad when we get the order to finally kill all those that claim to love God".

I said, "Ok, what do you want me to do?" He said, "I need you to go to Dallas Texas and pick up a computer chip for me". I said, "Ok", so he said, "Good I will have a friend drive you to the airport tonight, so get ready".

Well, I am flying to Texas just for a computer chip.

I landed in Dallas just fine and I was asked if I want to go to a party, so I went and it was so far in the desert, it seemed, but it was cool because they were shooting beer bottles and I said, "Isn't anyone afraid of the police showing up or the sheriff?" And so many just laughed at me because two guys from the border patrol were there having a good time.

Well, this guy known as The Wizard said, "This guy who is known as a spy came to investigate satanic ritual crimes so we had a surprise for him. See, the spirits channel unless someone is under that special protection we can know exactly who that person is and what they are doing.

They told this guy to park his car near this huge cactus plant and he did, then some guys and I were walking over to him and offered him a line of meth, he said, "No, I don't do that crap", so I knew something was wrong. They then said to him, "Share some drinks with us" and he said, "No, I just want to hang out". Then in a split second his legs were both shot each with a 357 mag. Then this one guy put a gas can in the car. I couldn't see what he was doing and then I heard, "Run!" And all of a sudden the car was exploding and anyone who was near it was gone as well. I have never seen a car explode before but it was so incredible".

Then the Wizard said, "Right when the car exploded 150 miles away his home was having a home invasion and everyone in the house was killed and his computer had gas poured all over it and then they lit it up. So we didn't care who sees what we did, we just want that computer destroyed. See, my friend, no matter what you do to one person, most likely it is a killing, to where everyone must act like a rattle snake and act quickly and deadly all at the same time".

As the night went on we went to a bar and it was fun. Then on the news it was reported that a house was broken into and they were killed with an axe and the computer room was totally destroyed by a fire and they were asking for help, wondering why anyone would do this? So if anyone has any information to contact the police. Then this reporter said what a horrible thing, but then several people were making the comments about how they want to kill him so I wondered would he be next?

Well I started to talk to the Wizard and he said, "That when people try to backstab or fall into the trap of thinking that they will be safe by letting the Feds know of all of our activities through integration and by joining a martial arts class, but sad fact is most don't get it, the beast will get you because he can find you even if you are in a metal box because it's not about what you see or feel or hear, it's a war of the minds.

People who decide to bring down a drug lord go into protective custody and live a happy and peaceful life for the rest of their life, but a person who exposes just a little bit suddenly falls in the shower in a cabin on a mountain somewhere a thousand miles in the woods, or out of nowhere a person that decides to expose demon worship goes into restaurant a thousand miles away and the restaurant blows up by a "so called" freak accident.

Ok, there was a time when a guy decided to expose a group of female prostitutes that wanted to get pregnant so that they could offer their baby to Satan, well as they were investigating his claim they had him three stories below the earth in a bomb like shelter, well a water pipe broke and this guy drowned because they locked the door and didn't tell anyone where he was and once again they claim it was a freak accident. See, my friend, the walls have eyes and the ground has ears so before warned".

Well I finally went to get the computer chip.

We got into a black Porsche and it was so very nice, I couldn't believe I was in this car. We went to a large soap distribution center that had thousands of cases of soap that would be delivered all over. This guy Mike and I got out of the Porsche and there were about six guys in a jet black Suburban following us. We drove the automobiles inside the warehouse.

There was a table that looked like a desk put in the corner of this place, they had just the one corner lit up so well but the rest of the warehouse was dark and we couldn't see a lot. We then approached this table and several of the guards came from around the corner, each one had a teardrop under their eye. And I noticed quickly that everyone I looked at had a tattoo of like a spider web on their left hand.

I realized by picking up this chip there was no turning back from this point, this chip had all the plans for those who were in great power throughout the world. It was a strange feeling knowing that what I was going to pick up could tell me who was going to be elected to be president, senators, congress, Supreme Court and rulers worldwide.

Well, as I stood there getting ready to be handed a chip, all of a sudden I was given a black book called "The Chip", at first I thought what is going on? But then I remembered my friend Pastor Ted, said nothing appears as it is and everything has a code, so remember live by codes not by names.

Well the book was inside a box that looked just like a case of hand soap and so I picked it up and then they said, "Ok, now put the book back in the case, seal it with this tape. Now, my friend, swear that if the tape is pulled on for any reason you are going to die, ok, and this book must be protected at all cost, so nothing can happen to this book. So if you know that you are going to get caught put this vile of acid on the book because nothing can stop this acid". Well, I was holding the box and we got in the car but before we left I had to swear to their terms so I said, "Ok".

Well we took off and ended up at a motel. We parked the cars in this motel parking lot and I thought we were going to walk in a room because each door had a number and I thought we were walking into room 13 but it was so bizarre, when we went in it was like looking at a huge place, it was very well hidden because when you first looked at it you saw the bed and then it looked like a light for the bathroom, just like a normal motel room, but this place as soon as you took a left which made it look like you were headed to the bathroom, there was no bathroom, you went right down a flight of stairs into a huge banquet room which led to other rooms. One of those rooms went into like a home theater room where it had a stage and several chairs that were all recliners so as to be comfortable.

Well, this guy, Shawn, yelled out and said, "Rick, there's a hidden room off to the left over there so put the box in there and come and follow me to this theater room", so I said, "Ok". There was cool 80s rock music being played. We then sat down and these pole dancers came out and were dancing all over. It was very cool to see and then someone was walking around wanting to know if you want a line of Coke or a drink, well I always did like Southern Comfort, so I got a drink.

While I was watching these girls I realized most of my life is just a fantasy, nothing seems real. It's so odd I have always wanted to find love and acceptance but this is all about power and how to get more of it. So many admired my position but I want someone to just love me for being me.

Well as the night went on I tried to figure out where do I fit in life? So I once again decided I need to take my life. Nonstop, I have constant thoughts that torment me, I wonder will I ever be loved and accepted? Does love really exist and will I ever really be happy? I ended up dosing off.

Well that party was wonderful. I enjoy cocaine so much I wish I could live in that state of mind all the time. I just feel so empty. It's amazing I have some of the world's most powerful Satanists and witches trusting me to transfer important papers and data, I can have sex with so many women or men and I can get drunk every night and go to a different party nightly but why am I feeling so empty? Isn't there something that I can do or some place I can go to find peace, joy, acceptance and love?

CHAPTER 14

Well after spending time away from home I was glad to be back. Things were fine on the surface but my drinking and meth use were getting so much worse now, I knew I was spinning out of control so I contacted a witch I knew and she said, "Let's see what the spirits say", so we put our hands on an Ouija board and immediately we knew the spirits were active but we wanted an ancient spirit to arise, so as the board was a on the table, I told Liz, my friend, who was the witch, to just step back, so I pulled my pants down and masturbated on the board, Liz then cut her tongue with a razor, mixed her blood with her spit and then let her spit flow like a river over the board to where it was long and looked tasty. Then she cut some of her hair off and some of my hair off and we placed it on the board, then all of sudden she said, "Throw dirt in my eyes to where tears will flow and it will hit the board". Well, as her tears were coming down and hitting the board the spirit said, "Liz stand over the board and pee on it", so I lifted Liz up and she was over the board and peeing on it.

Then she jumped down and the spirit said, "Now mix it together", so I mixed everything on the board together. The spirit then said, "Lick it up as if you were a dog", so I began to lick the board and this spirit that looked just like a wolf came out and said, "I am a spirit of deception and falsehood, I love telling people that there's hope just so I can watch them live a lie, so I can crush them so they will take their own life".

Then this spirit that looked just like a golden snake came out and said, "I am the spirit of blind concepts, I love causing people to think their skin color or they are so special themselves, that their race or their tribe is so important that they are above others. I offer false visitations and false signs from above to deceive people into thinking they are in contact with their ancestors."

I then saw the board turn all black and then the letters on the board appeared and it began to spell names and it said, "Speak my name", so I saw the name "Doo-law", I thought, "What is this"? Then immediately a tiny worm appeared out of an apple and said, "I went into the veins of Eve and I am the one responsible for deadly diseases. I love watching people suffer and they keep buying this or that trying to get better but it's because of the curse that God put on the earth that I came up out of the ground and now I destroy humans and animals, eating their flesh from the inside out".

Then this spirit said, "Look at the hospitals worldwide, people are dying from this and that but my favorite is America, so many are dying of cancer and so many don't realize that what they call a stress reliever or they call just a social thing, cigarettes, are filled with me and so at any time you feel fine then you die all because of something you claim made you feel good. Why did God create you stupid worthless things? So many are dying and blaming God but the funny thing is they did it to themselves, isn't that funny?"

I said, "I need help, I don't have a purpose to my life, will you help me?" And this spirit said, "You have been called to send the message out worldwide that God offers no hope and has too many rules". Then I saw like a black fungus come out of the board and it said, "If anyone puts their foot on the ground where I land this person will die".

Then the ground shook and I heard an awful sound and then it was quite. So Liz said, "Can you stay with me?" So I ended up staying with Liz for the night and then the next day I went home.

Well about a week later I threatened to kill my friend so I was locked up again in another psychiatric ward. I find it amazing; I wonder what is reality at times? Sometimes I just want to kill everyone and just have a good time blowing people away. But will this bring me any fulfillment in life? Well finally after being locked up for three months I finally convinced the staff I wasn't insane.

Well several of my friends decided to have a keg for me, it was so great and I was having the time of my life, a good friend bought me enough Coke so I could do a 3 day runner { STAY HIGH ON COCAINE FOR 72 HOURS} well I was doing ok till I came down, I saw ants the size of cars coming after me and I got my hands on an axe and I was trying to protect my own car from these things while screaming at the top of my lungs, "Let's rock".

Well I knew that I was in trouble this time because I woke up handcuffed to my bed and my ankles strapped down. I convinced the doctor and the psychologist that I had got some bad drugs and I was ok and not insane. After taking several tests that I barely past later on, I found out that I was almost committed to an insane asylum. So after being locked up for six weeks I was free again.

CHAPTER 15

A good friend came by and told me that a good friend was killed in a car accident so her brother took his life and then his girlfriend took her life, plus Peter, the coke runner, was caught with an ounce so he was locked up. So things weren't looking good at all, so that's when I decided it is time to really take my life.

Well I attempted suicide again and to my amazement I lived. Why? What possible reason could there be that someone like me would live? Why? On one hand is it the number of people that find any value in me?

Well as time went on I realized that I have a bad drug and alcohol habit but they seemed to be my only friends because I love Coke so much I would have sex with it if it asked me and I love being drunk. So I finally ended up in a rehab. I was doing great for about 65 days and then I knew I just had to drink.

I got a call from my pastor asking me where have I been, well I told him I was hiding out because I don't know how to act, talk or be now that I have given up everything.

Pastor said, "That's great but it is time to get back into things, I need you to fly to Birmingham Alabama and meet with some people who have some information that I need because remember even the president of the United States, congress, senators, C.I.A, F.B.I and even religious leaders have mainly decided that for the greater good of all mankind we must work towards a new world order and accept that the bible is weak and has too many faults and that the concept of trusting in a God that we can't see, and really know if it is Him speaking or not. So we must put our faith and trust in those who can communicate with the ancient gods, the stars, the earth, the wind and the bull, which is the right hand of the beast. These top 13 men are our living gods, they all have fame, wealth, popularity, respect and they all are in control of what we eat, drink, watch, see, hear, and what we can and cannot do.

I was so amazed, as long as you claim you are a religious leader and have wealth people will almost worship the ground you walk on. Well, I asked my pastor, "What day do I need to leave?" And he said, tonight", so I got my stuff together and then a black limo pulled up and I knew that things were getting intense because I heard music that I have never heard before, I heard the name of Christ being mocked and I heard so much hate in this song.

The driver said, "I heard you are the one who was asked to attend the meeting as just a witness, there will be 13 witnesses, 13 generals and 13 hosts who will run errands and get you anything that you need. But the grand total of people who will hear what is said in the meeting is 666, so there will be so much testing equipment to make sure all 666 people will hear what is being said. Remember to have fun because you never know what type of war goes on in the heavens when the greatest of Lucifer's generals come together".

Well we made it to the airport and the private jet was there and as soon as I got on the plane these people knew how I liked my coffee, plus they had a huge plate of shrimps for me. My flight was only about two hours so I just relaxed and looked out the window, nobody was allowed to ask me any questions and I could not talk to really anyone because their identity was all private.

My plane arrived and I was told that my clothes will be put away for me in the hotel room and would I need anything? Would I like to have any snacks put in the room?

Well the meeting started at 6 pm and this woman who was known as The Black Widow declared that for the next two years witches and true blooded Satanists will be praying to almighty Lucifer for the spirits of gossip, strife and control to destroy churches throughout America that actually read the Holy bible, that all "so called" Christian marriages would come under severe attack, children under the age of five would be abused and murdered at alarming rates. Worldwide anyone who claims that name, "Jesus Christ" would come under attack. The spirits of lack, diseases, and poverty would be free to roam and destroy. The spirit of greed would be loved and accepted throughout America especially and worldwide. "So called" Christians in America would become complacent, lazy, lukewarm, arrogant, and self-seeking."

Then after this black witch was done speaking, this guy got up and was dressed in a really nice suit and tie, who owned several TV and radio stations, said, "We are praying for more writers to come forward that will mock God, mock Jesus, make jokes about prayer and mock the Bible nonstop.

Then a man by the name of The Grand Dragon stood up and said, "If we can control all educational aspects, Math, Science, History, English and educational films we can implant all of our ideas into children. Then the child goes home and shares little by little with adults and pretty soon what we are teaching the children will be promoted on cartoons, commercials, movies, songs, newspapers, magazines, and talk shows. Remember children are young adults so we need to promote just that".

I am tired of seeing young girls in a one piece bathing suit, if we want to promote sexuality we need to promote young girls in bikinis. Also why does lingerie have to be a taboo thing? Let's make lingerie seem like something to wear around the house at night or something comfortable to still wear to bed, it will still promote a strong sexual appetite but our focus will be on something casual. Don't worry as long as we lie to people enough times, claiming lingerie can be worn as just casual clothing for at night and we just keep saying this, then we put it in sitcoms, and we advertise it in magazines, don't worry we will have people wearing lingerie all the time and even to work at times.

Look at how many beautiful women we have convinced that by starving themselves to death they are beautiful and even though we have had several die, look at how many want to take their place. It's funny if an animal shows its rib cage they call it animal cruelty and someone is either fined or goes to jail but if we help a young woman starve herself to the point of death the media calls her beautiful and we make millions".

Well then to my shock a religious leader got up and said, "We must convince people that there is no hope, so many are so terrified of this concept of U.F.Os or Big Foot, I am deeply impressed because I didn't realize it is so powerful to instill fear into people. Since I have been sharing the concept that there will be a food and water shortage, it would be a good idea to help the church build a shelter to store food, clothing and water.

Plus, ever since I quit preaching on sin, the Cross, the Blood, Jesus Christ's name, humility, being humble, the resurrection, the power of God, the Holy Spirit, praying in the spirit, Hell or loving God, did you know that my church is now mega? It is incredible, I am teaching people how God is a good God, so be happy and understand being gay is normal for some of you. Or ever since I started teaching on your own needs and wants need to come first it's amazing how my church is growing so fast. I just have to throw some scriptures out there and convince the people that they are good and living a blessed life and, wow, so many are almost begging me to accept money from them.

The other day I had a person come to me after I got done preaching and say I really need to repent because I have messed up badly and I said, my friend, repentance is gone, God knows your heart so you don't need to repent any more.

It was weird, after this religious leader was done speaking I wanted to vomit, I didn't know why but I felt that this religious leader was so far off from any truth, but why would I feel this? Who am I to question a religious leader?

Then this guy came forward fully decorated and had more medals on him than I could ever imagine anyone having to put on, it must take this guy 30 minutes just to put them on. He said, "I am honored and grateful to be here, I am General Thorn and I am here to tell you about the secret army that I am building, see so many ask me how can you get people to turn against their own family and friends but it will be easy, when people hear the word "Tripto", I then will control everything they do.

So many people have handed over their will by accepting a check that was clearly stated, "If you will accept this check for a thousand dollars we want to put a chip in you", and so they sold their being over to the beast and at the end of a meeting with these people they gave allegiance over to the beast. So the hour and time and day will come and I will control their minds and have them do battle for us".

Then he said goodbye but we must work together for the great day of the beast to be loved and worshiped.

Well I was glad it was over I just wanted to go back home and pretend to be dead because I realized that there really isn't any hope for me, I am just an average day guy who had no real hope of accomplishing anything, plus I haven't been blessed with intelligence or I am not very good with my hands. So after the meeting was over I was so grateful just to go to the airport. People are so blind to the concept of the new world order.

Well as I was there at the airport I was wondering, won't people be afraid of evil or run from it, so why would anyone want to be a part of it? Then all of a sudden I saw a music video come on the TV set at the airport and it was so pleasing to watch and then the announcer said, "Can you believe this, this girl looks like she's in her early 20s but in real life she is only 14?"

Then it hit me so hard, it was like someone just slapped me in the face, when the time comes to worship the beast it isn't going to appear to be evil at all but it is going to appear as a loving thing to do. It's odd, but look at how many times people said, "Well in my heart I felt it was the right thing to do". I get it now, "What happened to integrity, morals, values and ethics?" So many use every excuse they can of why they don't walk in integrity, humility and morals but I realize now that what so many people believe isn't because that's what they really believe, it is because they see it everywhere all the time so they think it's normal.

Well I was on the plane finally and I had a bizarre dream that an angel was sitting there all dressed in really bright white clothes and was telling me all about the power and love of Jesus Christ and I was in awe that Jesus Christ would have an angel tell me about His love for me considering I am a very evil and wicked person.

So I just thought this was a joke, I didn't think much of it but as we were getting ready to come in for landing the flight attendant said, "The man sitting next to you in the white suit, do you know what happened to him? We were wondering if you knew where he was because we are needing to buckle up now and I noticed both bathrooms were empty". Well I thought that is just wow, so I got off the plane and headed towards my car.

As I was walking through the airport I heard over the announcements, "It is a beautiful night, may the new world order begin soon". That made no sense, why did they say that? What was the purpose in that? That really bothered me so I went to security and said, "This is silly, why did the announcement say anything about the new world order?" And the guy said, "Go on your way or you will be arrested", then I remembered in the meeting the man said just keep saying it and people will believe it and accept it.

So I finally made it to my car and wondered, is it just me or does it appear that someone or something doesn't want anything that has to do with Christ or God in our society?

Then I finally made it home and turned on the news and the first thing I saw was that prayer groups were banned because they said these people were disrupting others. But I thought is this really happening everywhere? I look and listen and it amazes me how God, Jesus, morals and ethics are constantly being attacked. But why doesn't anyone question any of these so called leaders?

Then I decided it was time to jump into the shower. I then went out and decided I needed to go to a bar and just have a beer, but as I was watching the people, everything those leaders were talking about I could see was happening to the people. The more these people would say this or that it would happen, the more the spirit of perversion and self-centeredness controlled people to where they didn't care about people, they just wanted their needs met first.

Well a friend came over and I said, "I don't want to be alone tonight" but it was weird because I wasn't in the mood just to have sex with a woman because I thought what if there was more to life than just a good time? What if I had a purpose to this life?

So my friend said, "Well, can I sleep on your couch?" So I said, "Yes" and we left and she followed me in her car but before I went home I stopped and bought some beer and some munchies and then, wow, it just hit me, "Do I always have to eat munchies with beer or was that put in me by watching a commercial?"

So we finally made it back to my place and my friend said, "You know what, it's sad that these commercials make you believe if you wear their makeup, drink the right beer and have a tiny body you can have a wealthy, good looking guy at any time". Then I realized I wasn't the only one, so I wondered how many see all the lies? Well my friend just fell asleep on the couch, so I just went and crashed out for the night. I got up and realized my friend had left; she left me a note saying goodbye.

CHAPTER 16

I got a call from my friend, he asked me if I want to go to a concert so, I said, "For sure", I knew this was going to be a lot of fun so I said, "Yes", he said, "Great see you in about three hours".

Well I couldn't believe it, going to see a whole bunch of bands at one time. Dave came by to get me and we left, he said, "You wouldn't believe it, my place stays clean because I let different chicks crash on my couch while I am at work or at a party". So we just talked back and forth

Dave said, "I got some Coke for us, and get this, I finally was able to get some Ice", well I was all excited but I was also a little bit nervous of smoking or shooting ice so I just thought I will wait. So Dave said, "In my pack of smokes up there on the dashboard is filled with speeders if you want them", so I grabbed them and took five hits, I knew my heart was speeding now and it felt great, so I grabbed a beer from behind the seat and felt like this was going to be an awesome night.

We got to the parking lot and we had to walk to the gate to go into the concert and Dave said, "When we go in I need to find a place to shoot up because I can't wait to finally do Ice". We got inside and there was this back area behind a security wall and Dave shot up and then we went inside. It was wild, the music was so loud and there were so many people acting insane and a chick was being raped but that's nothing very uncommon at this type of event, besides she will just wake up from her high and think she had a good time.

Well the bands began to start and there was a heavy metal electric guitar war and that was so awesome and the crowd just went nuts and I looked at Dave and he said, "I am doing ok but I need a drink", so he went to go and get a drink. By the time the third song was being played I realized Dave must have gotten together with one of his exes or found a new babe, so I just had a great time around a whole bunch of people I didn't know.

I looked up on the stage and I saw dead people that looked all lost and confused and then everyone looked normal so I thought, wow, it must be the speed but then I looked again and I heard this as clear as day, "If they only would come to know me and realize I love them". Well it really scared me because how could I hear that as clear as someone talking to me at a loud banging concert with people screaming and yelling?

I decided I wanted to leave so I went to look for Dave, but just as I was looking for Dave this girl, Dove, saw me, so I said, "Hi'" and she said, "I am hungry we should go eat", so we went to get some food and we ended up at an Italian restaurant.

While we were looking at the menu I asked her, "Do you believe you have a purpose in life?" And she said, "Yes, I like taking care of handicapped people, you know I am divorced and I have a special child". I said, "Really? "That gives you fulfillment?" And she said, "Well I like sex a lot", but I said, "No, be serious". She said, "What do you want? We are here to just die", so I asked, "Well, what do you think about God?" She said, "I am a Christian because I believe in God". But then she laughed and said, "Do you honestly think God, being so great, would care about trash like us? We are all trash". I said, "Well, I thought He might".

She then said, "Do you realize almost every woman you know has been raped, several of our old friends are either dead from suicide or a drug overdose and, look, you even have an ex-girlfriend in prison, so please don't try to convince me God cares about you or me". Well we finally ordered and we got our meals and Dove said, "You need to stay off the hard drugs, they mess with you way too much". She then said, "Where do you need to go?" I said, "Just back home". She said, "Oh come on, we have to have sex it's been so long, so let's just do it"

So we got to my house and I had a message on my voicemail from the Emergency room, Dave had overdosed so Dove and I went to the E.R. and Dave was in a really bad shape, the doctor said he barely made it but he has to go to jail because he had a very dangerous drug in him.

So we went back to my place and Dove and I had sex, it was great but I thought what am I doing? I am just banging another woman, isn't there anyone that will fall in love with me or is love even true?

So I went and got into the shower and Dove was asleep on my bed. I held her all night long and I felt secure in that so the next day I said, "Let's go out for breakfast and I think we should start dating" and she said, "No way, I don't want someone that has such a rough past, and no joke, but Rick I don't like your friends and I don't even know what in the hell you do in life". So she headed towards the door and said, "Hey, for a good time you are great but I will never be with you because you are out there, at times I can see evil in your eyes", so she left.

I thought I need to go and get Dave's car, so I called a neighbor and said, "I need a ride to the Coliseum", so my neighbor came and got me. Well I got Dave's car, good thing that he left the spare under the tire and I took it to my house and I started cleaning it out and I saw that he didn't smoke or shoot all of the Ice he had, so I took it inside and I heard with an actual voice, "Don't do it!" Right then and there I knew I was going insane but then I thought, ok, if I am not going insane what is it?

CHAPTER 17

I heard this bang outside and I thought, "Ok, what in the world is that?" I looked out and I couldn't believe it, it was right where Pastor Mike was going to build his church.

Well, I walked over and I said, "Hi", and this man came over and said, "Hi", I said, "What are you guys doing?" He said, "Oh, I am the assistant pastor of God's army, it's going to be a non-denominational church, let me get you the pastor". So all of a sudden he yelled for Pastor Harley to come over. This pastor was over 6 feet tall and looked really intense and said, "Hi". But the way he looked at me and acted it was like he really did care, so I let them know where I live and that I might have to stop by some time.

Later on that day my pastor, Pastor Ted, called me and said, "My spirit guide is going nuts because there was a real Christian that was just up the street and I can still feel his presence, it is so powerful and we need to stop it because that group is dangerous". So I said, "Ok". Then he was getting another call so he had to go but I wondered, "Why if the beast is so powerful why is he so scared and those guys were real to me and I could see it?"

Well I could hear them over there again and someone was knocking on my door and to my shock it was Pastor Harley, he said "Hey, we got some extra food and we are having a barbecue to feed those wanting to help out, so come over and hangout". I said,

"Listen, Pastor, I appreciate you but your beliefs are totally different than mine and your God would just laugh at someone like me, so no offense but you should reach out to someone who is by far better than me". Well, Pastor Harley just said, "Come on over and get a burger", so I did. I couldn't believe it; the more I rejected this guy the more he reached out to me.

Well, as I was sitting there people were just hanging out asking me about life and people really were treating me like a friend. I couldn't understand why these people were so different, why would they accept me? Why don't these people fear me or fear the evil presence around me?

I told Pastor Harley, "I hope to come back again and thanks so much". Well I realized that none of the pastors that I have met were real pastors at all so I called Pastor Ted and said, "You are not a real pastor because I met the pastor who is going to be building his church on the corner and he was interested in knowing me".

Pastor Ted said, "You don't realize it but those people will try to brainwash you and try to convince you that their God, Jesus, is in control and has lots of rules". But I made it clear that I want those people in my life.

Then he said, "Rick, did you hear about Tony, he is suspected of being a serial killer but he isn't, he was just acting on what the spirits told him to do, so please we need your help to fulfill things for the glory of all men". Then Pastor Ted said, "Is it drugs, alcohol, more parties, sex, what is it that you want?" I said, "Acceptance with freedom", and then Pastor Ted said, "You will die if you continue on this road of nonsense".

So I got off the phone and I don't know why but I felt such a war going on inside of me, so I took a large butcher knife out of the drawer and I got down on my knees and I said, "I know this won't make sense to anyone but I am a living monster, I have done so many evil things that no matter what Pastor Harley or anyone says there's no way a loving God could accept me because I am the ultimate loser. My mother and father and almost everyone I have ever met have found no value in me or shown any love towards me at all. So many, even in high school, made bets I would die of an overdose on graduation night and the one person I deeply loved in high school who I would have loved to marry I threatened to kill".

Well as tears were running down my face, in one last silent plea to convince myself that maybe, just maybe I will find just 1% of value in me, I raised the knife to my neck and I was getting ready to shove it in there and I cried out to God saying, "Please forgive me for hurting so many people, forgive me for all of my mistakes and forgive me for being such a failure in life".

Then all of a sudden I felt these loving arms around me and for the first time I felt peace. Right then and there I knew I was set free from my drug and alcohol addiction and I was loved by someone. There are no words to explain it, there's nothing I can say to explain it, all I could do was sit there with a knife in my hands crying and praising Jesus Christ, I was free and I knew it. Well I got up but I just couldn't stop thanking Jesus Christ, I realized that Jesus Christ is alive, yes, he is alive and he really is our loving God!

Well I took the knife over to the sink and I saw the spirit of suicide and so many other spirits standing there mocking me and trying to convince me that I was worthless, so I began to wonder am I really forgiven? I also started to wonder should I take my life. And all of a sudden I heard, "Cry out to Jesus Christ for help". I did so and I was so blown away because even though I saw spirits that were shape shifters transforming themselves into snakes, werewolves, crows, owls and then ghosts, I thought I should be terrified but I am not, I have peace. Then I realized it's all about Jesus Christ being lifted up.

CHAPTER 18

Well, I called Pastor Harley and he said, "I will be right there" and he came over with another guy and they hugged me and we all said the sinners prayer together and then Pastor Harley said, "Can I pray over you?" Well as Pastor Harley and his assistant prayed over me, you could hear an awful noise like a pig being tortured and it came out of me and then all of sudden I heard, "Why do you hate us so much, why can't we stay here? You need us and we love you". Then I heard like a dam of rushing water say, "This is my son whom I love, release him now in Jesus Christ's name", at that moment I saw the finger of God point right at me. For the next hour all I could do was sit there holding Pastor Harley.

Then Pastor Harley's assistant said, "I am going to go and pick us up some pizzas", so he took off and I felt as if I was washed and I felt so alive. When his assistant pastor made it back we all ate.

Then Pastor Harley said, "Let's anoint your home", so he started praying over all the doorknobs, light switches, doorways, plus he put oil on the bottom of his shoes and said, "Jesus Christ, what an honor it is to be used for your glory", so he walked around to each room and asked Jesus Christ to anoint his shoes to where the power of God would flow, wherever his feet step down and whatever his hand touches, Jesus bless it and may your power flow".

I said to Pastor Harley, "Why were so many afraid of me that claimed to be Christians?" And he said something so shocking to me, he said, "Rick, so many like that title but they are phonies and so many are cowards but most are just what I call babies in the faith, they claim how they have been saved for so many years and that they have attended this or that school or teaching, but their faith is just a joke, they have no idea who they are in Christ and so all their head knowledge, is just that, it's all in their head. But to be mature in the things of God and to walk in the power of God isn't based on how many years you have been saved or what class you have taken, or who your pastor is, it is based on what do you believe.

See, read this; Numbers 14:24; "But my servant Caleb, because he has a different spirit in him and has followed me fully now" Pastor Harley said, "Stop. Do you see what God is saying? God made it clear that Caleb didn't list all the great things he has done or all the education that he has, He said Caleb had a different kind of a spirit, he followed after God fully".

Pastor Harley then said, "So many love to talk about how much education they have, how smart they are, how much money or success they have but unless you are giving all glory and praise to Jesus Christ you are being blinded and you are really being deeply deceived because life isn't about you, life is about Jesus Christ. See, so many "so called" Christian leaders are just as blind as those deep in the occult or Satanism. I have been to countless churches to where the people were being destroyed by demons and demonic attacks and yet the pastor would claim behind the pulpit how much the people were blessed and how great this body is, which is just so many countless lies.

See Rick, so many judge God and Jesus Christ so quickly but so many can't fathom just how much God's heart or Jesus Christ's heart is breaking because He loves us so much and He deeply desires to have a relationship with us so badly.

So many don't realize this but when you have encountered the love of God you will never be the same again. So many people send me letters asking for prayer, texting me, e-mailing me, coming to the church, calling me or sending me messages on social network pages asking for prayer but it is so sad because so many of these people battle with this and that and I just want to hold them all and say it's the love of God that breaks the chains of bondage. See, the love of God is so deep and tangible, yes you can feel it and you can breathe it in, it is really that deep.

I have been to a worship conference where I could not even stand because the presence of God was so strong, I just had to be on my knees crying and thanking God for who He is.

So many ask me why is it so many fall away or battle with sin for years? I explain to them that when you encounter the love of God your heart melts and you feel the love of God like a warm blanket being put around you and you know that when you encounter the love of God chains are being broken and you are no longer a prisoner to sin.

When someone says how can Christians commit evil deeds or torture someone, or even beat a child to death, it is because so many are bound by religion. But when you encounter the love of God you will never be the same. See, when you encounter the love of God you just know you are not the same. So many judge God or Jesus Christ so quickly that they refuse to ever go to church again or read their bible ever again.

But here's a sad fact, even if someone well-known like an athlete or someone well-known in Hollywood abuses or rapes someone they are still worshiped and loved, plus so many still want their autograph. All because God didn't answer every little whim a person has they walk away from God but if a famous person was to ignore them they would still worship and admire them.

It bothers me because God's heart is breaking and He wants to be a part of your life but so many ignore His cries but then turns around and claims to be a Christian.

Just quoting scriptures and going to church on Sundays but never really understanding the heart of God is not enough. God wants to hear about your day. God wants you to tell Him about your job, what scriptures you like.

It is just so sad because so many make fun of children and the way they pray but God wants His children to be like a child when it comes to building a relationship with Him. Why is it silly to ask God if these clothes match? Or why is it silly to ask God for a bigger or smaller truck or car? See, God doesn't want a bunch of robots just saying I love God and I memorized another scripture today. What if all those who claimed to memorize this or that scripture actually believed what they memorized?

See, Rick, it's by no accident that you got saved after all you have been through because God has a plan and a purpose for your life".

Then to my surprise Pastor Harley wanted to share one more lesson with me which I am so glad about because I needed to hear all this and I didn't know that this lecture would stay with me for the rest of my life; he said, "I want to share one more thing with you, which I will warn you about, it's called "legalism", these are people who have no solid evidence of what they are saying, they like to take just one or two scriptures out of the bible and say the bible says this so there's nothing to discuss. It's very sad because these people are full of themselves, argumentative and many times claim how they have gone through this or that training but what these people lack is humility.

You will find out that humility is very important to God, humility goes before honor, but pride goes before a fall. So many who fall into legalism become so blinded that they are so entangled with the spirit of religion that they can't and will not accept anyone's opinions unless it is 100% in agreement with theirs.

There was a group of men called the Pharisees who were very respected and knew the law, they are the ones who convinced the crowd to crucify Jesus. These were the "so called" experts of the word of God but were so blind that they couldn't see that the spirit of religion had them all bound up. See these people love to shout out smoking cigarettes is evil and you can't be saved but the number one cause of death is being obese which is from eating too much and being lazy.

Now I am not trying to tell anyone to go out and smoke but I believe too many pastors and leaders walk in too much fear from the truth. It's so sad so many leaders, yes leaders, would rather have their friends, staff and congregation burning in a lake of fire than offend them and confront their sin.

When I had a pastor exposed of being gay it shocked so many but I wasn't at all surprised because too many would rather be a man pleaser and get their pay check than confront a leader in the church of sin. So many claim you have to wear a tie, dress up, drive a nice car, live in the right neighborhood, have the right job and be part of the right ministry but Jesus made it clear to so many, "I never knew you so be damned". What shocks so many is Jesus loves the poor, the prostitutes, the drunks, the needy, those that have got head lice and those that smell like a cigarette".

Well, Pastor Harley left and I could tell I really did encounter the love of God, I want to know Him and I want to know what is in the heart of God.

CHAPTER 19

T hen all of a sudden it was like a tidal wave that came over me and the Spirit of God said, "Take out a piece of paper" and said, "I want to teach you and help you, so write these things down;"

Love is not being controlled, called filthy names, love is not slapped, cussed at, spit on, punched, kicked, laughed at, made fun of, ridiculed, beat on, have your hair pulled out, being degraded, being made to feel worthless, being forced to have sex, being raped, being burned, being forced to sleep in a dog pen, being forced to sleep in a garage, being withheld food, sleep, clothes, being forced to surrender all your money or your worldly possessions ,feeling threatened, being manipulated, being lied to, being used, being forced to eat dog or cat food, being cut, being knifed, burned, tortured, being forced to suffer, being forced to wear a dog chain or dog collar, being sodomized, being drugged, forced to lose weight, threatened, being forced to do anything that is mentally, emotionally, psychical or spiritual that is harmful to you or life threatening. Being forced to do anything that you feel is mentally, emotionally, spiritually or psychically wrong. Also love is not a being a punching bag for anyone. Being told you need to lose weight or you need to change the clothes you wear, or the way you are, and love is not staying with a spouse that cheats on you with other women or men.

Then I heard the Holy spirit say here's what love is; it is kind, does not envy, does not parade itself, it is not puffed up, thinks no evil, does not behave rudely, does not seek its own, it is not provoked, does not rejoice in iniquity, rejoices in truth, bears all things, believes all things, hopes all things, endures all things. Then the Holy Spirit said, oh how excited and happy I am to share with you the love and awesomeness of who Jesus Christ is.

Then I realized wow this is true, I really am in the presence of God, oh, what a loving God he is.

Then I asked the Holy Spirit, "When I was heavy into Satanism I was always shocked how many people would claim how awesome their God was and how powerful God was. In restaurants or school and, yes, even in church I would walk up to people and ask them about God or Jesus and over and over again people became terrified or very fearful of me so I really believed that Lucifer had so much more power. I could never understand why anyone would want to be a Christian when all I saw was cowards, fear and so many self-righteous people, so many are so self-righteous that they can't see that so many are on their way to Hell, but they are more concerned about how the person is dressed before reaching out to them".

The Holy Spirit said, "Most people who claim to know the love of God are on an emotional feel good concept about God and the power of Jesus but it's a roller coaster ride. One day a week they want to serve God but then the next day or week something else comes along.

So many of God's people walk in ignorance and defeat because their own leaders don't know how to walk in the power and authority of Christ. It's time to come to know Jesus, the real King of Kings and Lord or Lords. God almighty is shaking the fence and so many don't know what to do but the hour is now to either get excited about the things of God and run to the battle or be a coward and live in defeat. So many will say don't speak against this or that and don't proclaim this or that but no matter what they say they fear offending people. As soon as you say anything from the word of God you will offend someone, so speak the word of God".

I was amazed that the Spirit of God being so Holy and loving would want to know me. Well I had to think now about my new life, what will I do, or where will I go, to school or work?

CHAPTER 20

Well the following Sunday I had it arranged that Pastor Harley was going to pick me up so I could go to church with him till his new church got built close to my home. Well I went to church and it was exciting hearing the word of God being preached and taught with so many people wanting to learn and grow in Jesus Christ.

It was really exciting because as I was sitting there, Pastor Harley was preaching a message called, "Not my will but Your will be done". He pointed out that Jesus was continually making it a point to do the will of the Father, but then he said, "Most Christians think Satanists are those that wear black clothing and go to sex orgies but to be a real Satanist it is seeking after what you desire not what God desires. In the world of Satanism you will hear these words, "DO what thou wilt shall be the law", see, he is pointing out do what you want to do. So many commercials and sitcoms love saying do what you want, do your own thing, your way is best, have it your way, you deserve to have everything you want, but what about your creator?

See, you can do it your way but when the hour stops and it's your time to stand before Jesus will He even know you? So many can't fathom just how awesome Jesus Christ is and just how much He really loves them. See, Jesus didn't have to die on a cross or go through severe agony for you or I but Jesus looked up to the Father and said, "Not my will but Your will be done".

So many have said God spoke to me about being on the mission field or getting into the ministry but my mom, dad, sibling, grandparent, friend or my spouse talked me out of it but ask yourself this; "Who will you answer to?" So many have said God spoke to me about writing a book, starting a band, singing songs, being a worship leader. See, when you say I am praying about it that's great but personally I think that has turned into the biggest copout I have ever heard. Church it's time to get right with God He loves you and wants to bless you".

Well, after being saved and having a real relationship with Jesus Christ, Pastor Harley asked me to study Scripture on being water baptized, so after studying them and really deciding I need to do this it was so exciting to pick a date to finally be baptized. So about three weeks later I was baptized and then that night they had a big dinner for all those that were baptized. It was so awesome to be part of a family and have people really care about me just as a person.

Then Pastor Harley said, "Ok, all those that haven't been baptized in the spirit let's do this now" and all of a sudden some awesome music was playing on the sound system and Pastor Harley yelled out, "Spirit of God power out your awesomeness". At first it was just so awesome knowing I was there being a part of this and then I realized, wow, something is happening because it was like a bulldozer was pushing back the enemy and all the darkness with such force you could feel the finger of God just pointing and darkness fled.

Later that night so many of us were heading out to go home and we noticed that dead animals were all over the parking lot and as you got closer to them they had satanic markings all over them. Then Pastor Harley said, "Jesus!" in a really loud voice, he then said, "Jesus protect this church, these people, this parking lot and let your glory come". Several people said, "Wow". I should have been terrified but I was not because I felt secure in the arms of God.

So we walked around the parking lot picking up dead animals and putting them in plastic bags and then after all of them were gathered Pastor Harley said, "Jesus, please bind up the power of the evil one and may all the evil that was spoken out as these animals were being murdered. I bind up right now in Jesus Christ's name and I cover my prayers in the Blood of the Lamb". Then Pastor Harley said, "Tomorrow we will bury them so let's just put them in the shed", so we did and then we left.

When I got home there was a bull's head on my front porch covered in blood so I called Pastor Harley right away and he told me some shocking news, "He said years ago when I was heavy into Satanism myself I was always shocked how many people would claim how awesome their God was and how powerful God was but when it came time to show love or compassion to someone that was into Satanism or an occult in a restaurant or at the college and, yes even in church, I would walk up to them to ask them about God or Jesus and say, "Do you believe Jesus has more power than Satan?" When they could see I was wearing a pentagram on my shirt over and over again these people became terrified and became cowards, fearful of even me, so I really believed that Satan had so much more power. I could never understand why anyone would want to be a Christian when all I saw were cowards and so many self-righteous people.

"See Rick, everyone wants people set free and everyone wants to see people get saved but they are just like the Pharisees, they are lazy or fearful so they go to a feel good church to where the concept is let's not offend anyone or do anything to help anyone. But here is the problem; unless you are willing to get dirty you will never win any souls for the kingdom of God. Plus, if you don't get dirty you will never teach anyone how to win the battles they face. See, the feel good religion won't set you or anyone else free.

It's time to come and humble ourselves and ask, "Is life about me or about Jesus Christ?" Then Pastor Harley said, "Everyone says use me" but when God says, "Ok", they complain and get all upset because it wasn't the way they were thinking it should be. So many truly don't want to be used by God, they just want to soak up the blessings of God and be cowards.

I realized right then and there that if I truly want to know Jesus Christ I must give up all my hopes, dreams, desires, wants and needs to Him. I told Pastor Harley, "Wow, being a living sacrifice and to imitate Christ is nothing like those prosperity people preach about or one of those people who claim how they are part of a denomination but forget that being like Christ isn't carrying a 10 pound bible, dressing up in expensive clothes and being self-righteous".

Then Pastor Harley said, "Most people are lost just as much as the world is so if your pastor doesn't know how to walk in love, humility, power, authority and compassion run, yes run".

CHAPTER 21

W ell after being saved for two years I realized that too many were living in defeat and my heart just went out to them so I said, "Pastor Harley, teach me how to walk in power and authority so I can teach others" and he said, "Rick, before you teach anyone anything look for three master keys in a person's character and personality. These master keys will either help you walk right into the blessings of God or they will stop you from ever reaching the blessing of God".

So Pastor Harley said, "Key one, Being Faithful; is the person going to be faithful in doing what you ask them to do? Are they studying the word of God? Are they faithful to the church? Are they honest when someone says why do you believe this or that? Can you question them on why they read the books or magazines they read without them getting defensive? Can you question them on the movies or TV programs they watch?"

Then Pastor Harley said, "Key two, Accountability; are they reaching out to someone in the body that is walking in integrity, humility, love and wisdom? Are they willing to humble themselves and say can you help me?"

Then Pastor Harley said, key three, Are They Teachable? See, it's so stupid that so many are offended by some of the silliest things.

I have people who have just got saved attend my bible study and the "F" word is being used to explain something.

In the back of the building I really offend religious people because I allow smokers to smoke their cigarettes there.

Years ago, Rick, I attended a church that had a great pastor but the bishop was the overseer and so the church stayed lukewarm and did not have a lot of miracles or salvations. But being a great leader at times is admitting that you don't belong in your position.

Through the years of me being saved, less than 1% of all the churches raised up anyone and sent them out. If you are that afraid that your staff will fall if they are sent out why do you even have them as your staff? I have had two pastors fall into gay relationships and one of them had so much pride in himself that when he fell he still was so in love with himself.

I have also had a pastor divorce his wife and marry the secretary. So many times people say it won't happen to my pastor but over and over again so many men and women of God fall because they put their trust in the doctrine, how many scriptures they have memorized, their education, their pastor or their leadership when it is very clear we are supposed to put our hopes and trust in Jesus Christ. I have learned that most people are flaky that's why it didn't crush Jesus when they came to arrest him, not one apostle was willing to stand with him.

I once was going through a horrible time I just felt like Satan was nicer than the Christians around me that were mocking and judging me, I had so many coming against me. At one time I ended up being homeless in the middle of winter and lost all my friends. But even though I could have easily died Jesus Christ took care of me step by step. Eating just a simple peanut butter sandwich was a big deal. So no matter what happens realize that some of the worst enemies you could ever have will claim to love Jesus and they will act just like Judas.

After listening to Pastor Harley help me out I said, "Will you write out prayers for me to help myself and others who don't understand how to pray?" So Pastor Harley said, "Yes, I will help you". Well I said, "Pastor, I will see you probably tomorrow" and he said, "Great".

CHAPTER 22

I got a call from a really hot looking babe that I knew, that could make love to you one minute then rip your liver out the next and eat it. Lori was so hot but very evil and I knew that she had a lot of problems. She once said, "Can you believe it, Rick, when I saw a building getting blown up and bodies were lying all over and people were crying, I just sat there eating my lunch, then a person said you lack empathy and so I told my counselor this and she said it is true, Lori, you just don't seem to have emotions at times it is as if they are dead".

I said, "Hello, Lori" and she said, "Why aren't you around anymore? What has happened to you? We have been having so much fun and so many wild things are happening so please come to one of our parties". I said, "Ok, I will think about it but I have to go".

Well the next day I called Pastor Harley and let him know that someone from my past had called me and Pastor Harley said, "Let me tell you a story, ok? I am not here to judge you but did you see who Christ reached out to? The bible is very clear about this; that bad company corrupts good character but how can you expect a Satanist, a witch, a Tarot card reader, a murderer, psychic or medium to understand or discover the love of Christ?

See, several years ago when I was helping take care of this business I began to share my faith and one man began to tell me about his faith, well I was shocked when he shared his past with me because he was a recovering pedophile. So my faith was challenged, will I love this man? Can I care about this man?

Church it's time to ask ourselves are we really willing to walk in the power and love of Christ or is it just words but no action. We are told to imitate Christ but so many dress and act like the world, does Christ really live in our hearts or not? It is time to get off the fence. This is why I said to you before going to church isn't just so you can brag about your pastor or brag about your church and it isn't so you can win a prize. Going to church is so important because God never called anyone to be an island and God never said it's about you, your walk is about Jesus Christ.

Please also listen to this, so many people I have met through the years really believe that they are under demonic attack or under a demonic oppression but when most people go to a church faithfully and get involved and start helping someone else all of a sudden they notice that 90% of their problems go away. See, in today's life the TV, radio, sitcoms, music, movies, the internet and video games are mainly directed to make you feel better, giving you a false hope that you are in control and you deserve whatever you want.

It is so sad how many people really do believe that if they aren't being sexually satisfied all the time, if their spouse doesn't fulfill all their emotional needs, if their pastor doesn't talk about things that interest them all the time, if an evangelist doesn't take the time to say hi to them, if their favorite restaurant doesn't have their seat open, if their spouse is now ageing or gaining weight, if their bank won't give them a loan, or the church they go to doesn't buy them a lot of groceries, or God doesn't answer every prayer, or if I don't e-mail the person back, or I don't give my number out or call the person back this person just gives up on anyone and everything all because they feel that nobody cares. People like this live in a world of self-pity.

See, this might shock you but life isn't about you and all your needs. So if you want to experience joy and peace quit looking at your needs and why not be there for someone else? So many just want to find love and acceptance but these can only truly be found in Christ. So many pastors walk away from their calling, so many evangelists give up, so many leave the ministry because they were hoping that their education, their church, their beliefs could bring joy and peace but these things can only come from Christ.

Well after almost three years I am really beginning to understand how to walk in power, love and authority. It's so different being around a group of people that claim that they are so used to living with depression, sadness, defeat, worry, strife, anger, hopelessness, lack, poverty and need that they find Pastor Harley really shocking but within a short time they start living in freedom, so I hope I don't ever become stubborn and get offended and leave.

Pastor Harley loves to preach on this because so many get offended and just leave but the sad fact is many times people are offended by a simple misunderstanding. And now I also see it clearly, it has never been about religion or what bible you read out of, it has always been about Jesus Christ. It always shocks me when someone says my mega church has five thousand and yours has only three thousand so mine must be better.

Just then the Holy Spirit said, "The wicked praise, glorify one another but God's own people are caught up in competition". It just amazes me that I know very little but yet so many who have been serving Jesus Christ for 20 or 30 years stand in judgment because this or that person is doing this or that but when you ask them, "So what are you doing for the kingdom of God?" they get all offended.

When someone says I am too busy to help lead the evil out of darkness I really wonder if they even have a clue to what the word of God and Jesus Christ are all about.

I told Pastor Harley, "It's amazing that so many are so spiritually fat but they do nothing with it because they have become so complacent". Pastor Harley said, "If the church would ever grow up and realize Christians are under severe attacks we could take back our land, schools, homes, neighborhoods, streets, cities and states but the church has become so lazy that it's amazing when you meet just one Christian in a church that really does read their bible every day or prays every day, yes just one".

Well Pastor Harley had to and go and meet some people so I decided to just really begin to pray and started wondering where will I go in life? Since I had to study maps and locations of all over it's odd but I realize now I could go all over but I want to be in the Father's will.

The following Sunday Pastor Harley dropped the ultimate bomb on so many people; he said, "Why do so many Satanists pray every day but most Christians pray for just five minutes a week?" He said come on church, think about this, why do so many fear Satan or demons they have such faith that he can do this or that but a very little amount of Christians believe in the power of God. See, we spend so much time on the news, in music, in movies, in magazines, and TV, glorifying evil that people have now bought the lie that Jesus is weak and Satan is so mighty and to be feared. But after the dust settles and Jesus is on the throne what are you going to do or say? Church, it's time to start lifting up the name of Jesus Christ and start worshiping Him and praising Him.

Prayer is easy, talk to Jesus Christ, just talk to Him, He loves you and He would love to hear how your day is going. So many people think prayer should be done this way or that way but really why say dumb things that make no sense, pray to Jesus while you are lifting weights, while driving a car, while driving a forklift, while working on a crane, while driving a semi, while sitting behind a computer, if you are a cook why can't you talk to Him? If you are working construction why can't you talk to him?

See, you don't actually have to talk to God with your mouth, you can discuss life with Jesus Christ even in your mind. So many don't pray because they either take Jesus Christ for granted or they have no faith in Him. If you want to know the Jesus Christ I know just talk to me after the service, or if you want to know Jesus Christ or rededicate your life come forward". It was so awesome to see so many go forward seeking a true relationship with Jesus Christ.

After the service was over, I was thrilled to get the scriptures written down in my bible that followed today's service. Well I realize I have been called to help raise up an army for the kingdom of God but at the end of this book I will share with you warfare scriptures and prayers that will help you understand what warfare is all about. Be blessed........

CHAPTER 23

Well that afternoon after the service was over Pastor Harley got a call from one of the guys from the sheriff's office and said, "We are hearing about a ritual that will be taking place tonight". Pastor Harley got off the phone and told me the news and then he said, "So many people don't realize that even some of the most powerful men and women of God that you could ever meet are working in law enforcement and so many of them, yes do hear from God so they contact me to start praying".

Well, that night Pastor Harley had about 20 people from four small towns come together to drive around and pray from 9pm to 2am, it was exciting because I could feel it in the air, it was cold and heavy it was as if someone was going to die just to sacrifice a life for the beast. So I asked the pastor who I was assigned to be with because we always worked in pairs, never alone, then he said, "Stay with Pastor Tim, we are going to follow a certain car and so we did".

And I knew, it they were driving around speaking curses and I then saw the tape from a cassette on an antenna flowing all over as they were driving around.

"See, witches will have a coven record curses being spoken by witches on a cassette and then they will pull the tape out of it, wrap it around the antenna and then every time they go on a new street or an intersection they will say, "Release", this releases all the evil curses they spoke over the cassette.

For instance, anyone living on a street that starts with an "A" will suffer from anger, lack, frustration, worry and doubt but anyone living on a street that starts with an "E" will have thoughts of rape, murder, incest, divination, so see, this is how they destroy so many people, said Pastor Tim because most Christians don't even pray over their house so they surely aren't going to pray over their neighborhood. The sad fact is most pastors don't even pray over their parking lots or their building".

Well as we got close to the car I yelled out, "Jesus Christ, bind up all spirits from being released from that car". I was so amazed, just then the car quit working and pulled off to the side so we asked them if they needed anything and they gave us the satanic hand sign and just looked the other way. It was awesome to see God move like that so I said to Pastor Tim, "Wouldn't it be so cool if more Christians would humble themselves and seek the power of God?"

Well we knew that it was getting close to midnight so we all met at the edge of the forest and started worshiping and praising Jesus Christ.

So then Pastor Harley said, "You know that Hollywood like to tell us that evil only happens in the dark woods but just look at the police reports". So he said, "Ok, now we need to go to that supermarket off of Main and go into their parking lot and just praise God there also, since we know that they are closed nobody would even care".

Then Pastor Tim said to me, "Did you see that article about the psychics and mediums offering to go inside your businesses or homes for a fee and calm the spirits down but I would do it for free". Then he showed me their advertisement;

"Are you experiencing bizarre thoughts, strange things happening in your home? Are you having nightmares? Are you hearing voices? Are you being touched sexually in your sleep? Do you have thoughts of violence? Are doors opening and closing with no one around? Is water being turned on and off for no apparent reason? Is food rotting in your fridge when you know you just bought it? Do you see ghost or spirits? Contact me today and I will calm down the spirits in your home or business today for five hundred to a thousand dollars".

Then pastor Tim said, "So very few ministries are willing to reach out to satanists, occultists, witches, psychics, mediums, and those deeply involved in palm or body reading, voodoo, séances, and those seeking answers from Ouija boards and tarot cards. So many think God has given me a special faith or anointing to reach out to these people but I don't, it's called loving people because Christ died for them so who am I to judge them?" I was in awe knowing that this man of God really loved people because it saddens me how many in full time ministry want a person to look good, smell good, be stable, come to their church to get saved.

Well Pastor Harley and several police officers with all the rest of us were just in this parking lot with no one around just praying to the East, the West, the South and the North proclaiming that Jesus Christ is Lord. Just then there was a shaking in the spirit and I could tell so many people were being set free even while they were in their beds asleep.

Then one of the deputies got up and said, "So many people in prison, men and women have said I should have just walked away or I should have just got that thought out of my head. So many don't realize just how poisonous thoughts are till it's too late. The bible is very clear about casting down thoughts and imaginations but yet so many men and women are serving time for robbing a bank, killing someone, or stealing and so many are in prison because of drugs. So many just want a onetime escape, just a onetime relief, just a onetime experience and then find themselves hooked and now losing everything. As shocking as it sounds over and over again the person had a thought and before they knew it that thought became a reality.

So many cults actually were a loving church at first but once again when the person decided to think that they were the only one who had answers. So many people don't see value in themselves so they end up doing something they regret, so please reach out and share the love of Christ. So if you have a thought or a dream and it isn't lined up with the word of God cast it down. It's time to be like Christ! It's time we declare war in the heavens".

As this man was speaking so many began to cry knowing that any one of us could be in prison, in an insane asylum or Hell because we have all made horrible mistakes. Then Pastor Harley said, "So many Satanists, witches, those deep in cults, or those that belong to an occult, or like to play with Tarot cards, Ouija boards and those that are psychics, mediums, crystal ball readers or those that are into bizarre sexual things and, yes even those that worship a demon all need to hear there is hope and forgiveness in Jesus Christ. If we, as Christians, don't tell a dying world there's hope who will?"

Well we then all said good night and we all went home. I couldn't believe it, here it is 2:30 in the morning but I feel alive knowing I am doing something good for the kingdom of God. Well I realized now there is so much work to be done for the kingdom of God.

Well I enjoyed talking to Pastor Tim and so I got hold of him after work and we were discussing how many are really deceived. Pastor Tim said, "So many Christians have got the idea that any day now they are just going to round up all the Christians and kill them but so many don't realize that the beast is going to make it where people will fall away all on their own without a fight. As sad as it is to say so many have become so complacent and so in love with the things of this world that so many don't even know what truth is anymore.

See, if the enemy attacks the church there would be a great revival but if you slowly take away every Christian aspect from Christians most will just say, ok. The enemy is very smart, he's not saying kill Christians, the enemy is saying no bibles allowed, then no more honoring God, then it's now a law that you can't pray and in so many places now it is against the law to be poor or help the poor which God has asked all of us to help.

Little by little all of our rights are being taken away and so many are being trained or being conditioned for the arrival of the anti-christ. Sitcoms are mocking God and we call it just humor, Ouija boards and Tarot cards have become so popular and we claim it's just fun, games. And the logos that we put on T-shirts now are openly satanic and we just claim they are cool looking".

Well I said to Pastor Tim, "Let's go and get some lunch", as we were waiting for lunch I said, "I find it amazing how many people have said nobody is willing to discuss demons or warfare so they are grateful to be at Pastor Harley's church".

After lunch was over, Pastor Tim had to leave and plan a trip to Chicago.

CHAPTER 24

Well later on that day as I was praying, the Spirit of God was talking to me about exposing the darkness to Pastor Harley about praying for people and places, so I called Pastor Harley and we met up later that day.

I was explaining how on Black Friday most people see it as a day to shop and get great deals and so most Satanic covens will use this as a time to claim that a child for instance with black skin, wearing a blue jacket, wearing white tennis shoes must die before 1am, see, they make up games that are ruthless and evil just so they can experience a deeper evil with Satan.

It always amazes me how many Christians have got the concept, "If I don't see it I don't believe it", but yet every day hundreds of lives are being destroyed by demons.

Also there is an actual calendar called "The Witches Dates or The Satanic Calendar"; this calendar will give you dates and duties you must fulfill, so for instance if it says in the month of July find a red headed boy that can walk, have him as a sacrifice for midnight. So as soon as you see a child that has read hair, a boy that can walk, pick the child up and keep it safe for less than 30 days for the sacrifice. See most children are traumatized severely close to 30 days and don't see any of their family so they would be a reject to the enemy.

Also here's another example; three wealthy babies, yes they must be babies all from wealthy families, must all die three days before Easter Sunday. One night a contest from all the covens in Illinois will draw a pentagram over the state, anyone that lives in side of the drawing is forced to be in the contest so there's a lot of witches and satanists in these contests.

When black witches of any region want to put on a contest they can but if a certain amount of witches or satanists get caught committing a crime the black witch from that region will be tortured and not allowed to die for 33 days no matter how bad they are suffering they just wanting to die. So as bizarre as it sounds some witches were given vitamins or put in a hospital so they could go back to torturing them again after they got well. So if a contest is made you must do it or you can become a sacrifice victim or you will be executed when you don't even suspect it.

Well one night a black witch who got a ticket said, "Ok, 33 days ago I got a ticket at 8pm so after 8pm the first person to cause let's just say an accident and the police officer dies wins the golden prize".

CHAPTER 25

Well after several months of working with Pastor Harley trying to get information out there I discovered that since most of the information I know about isn't talked about much I would travel around sharing the truth with people.

So many people wherever I go are so interested in the paranormal shows but isn't it shocking how so many people have a real encounter with the paranormal go insane? It's odd, so many are so marveled by a chair moving, a desk shaking, a black figure moving, a door slamming but then when it happens to them they have no idea what to do so they fall right into the hands of the enemy, believing a medium or psychic has the answers or they put their trust in a Catholic priest, when there is only one name you can trust and there's only one name that can and will defeat darkness and there's only one name that is above every name and His name is Jesus Christ!

When a person claimed that they can throw salt over their shoulder I thought they were joking at first but then I realized they were serious, so I asked, "Do you believe that the under garments Mormons wear will protect them? Or a rosary will protect a catholic?" She looked right at me and said, "No", Then I said, "Ok". Then I said, "Show me in the bible where anyone threw salt over their shoulder. I said you won't find one because witches did this, never the Christians". I knew she was going to be very angry with me because when a demon has you convinced to do something meaningless he doesn't want you to let that worthless thought go because as long as you do anything that won't harm the kingdom of darkness all demons in Hell will try to make sure you believe in stupid lies.

It also amazes me how many people really think that when they have a medium or psychic come into their homes, the person is communicating with a dead person's soul, so many don't realize they are communicating with a demon not a person's lost soul. So many people will believe lies because someone else said it. But the sad fact is most "so called' Christians don't even know what they believe because so many leaders today in the churches are cowards and are lost themselves.

I have actually attended a church where the youth pastor was selling dream catchers. In another church freemasons could be welcomed freely and not once did the pastor ever speak against secret societies in fear of offending someone.

I have actually witnessed racism towards white people and black people in two different churches. I have seen a leader being gay. I have seen affairs and yes, I have even gone to churches where people who were supposed to be my leaders walk in fear of the enemy.

I wonder many times in prayer will the church ever wake up and realize we are in a major war or will the majority of the church just keep smiling and claim happiness while so many Christians are committing suicide, walking away from the gospel, getting a divorce just as fast as buying a marriage license?

As time went on I sat there in prayer wondering where do I go, Father in Heaven. So many are destroyed when their heart is breaking. Well as I was sitting there I got the biggest revelation of my life, I realized now that my life isn't about worrying about those lost in false doctrines, my life is to tell people that Jesus Christ loves them and His love is so thick and tangible that He really does want to know everyone deeply because He is a merciful, loving, caring, kind God that is wanting everyone to know Him, that He is so genuine and so real and He just wants everyone to know Him and see that He is a loving and caring God.

So as I began to share with people worldwide about the Father's love, I was so surprised when I found out that there's one big thing Christians and Satanists have in common and that is they believe that they are condemned. I have sat there and cried with countless people because they dont realize that the Father's heart is broken so badly because so many choose to believe in a lie rather than accept the truth that He really loves them and wants them to know Him. So my journey began telling people just how awesome and merciful God is.

CHAPTER 26

Well, as I began to travel and tell people about the love of the Father, I realized that so many believe in the Father's love but most people don't realize that if we don't acknowledge our sin then we will never get close to the Father because it was sin that caused God to ask His only Begotten Son to die on the cross for each and every one of us, so we must understand that it was the cross that allows us the privilege of getting to know the Father.

I never really realized just how much God loves me and when I began to realize that those who have been forgiven love so much. See, when I go and talk to crowds of people I really enjoy helping people understand that when you realize your sin put Jesus on a cross to suffer for you, you can begin to understand just how much the Father loves you. So when you finally humble yourself and ask God to forgive you for your sin you begin to realize that even though you have committed so much evil and wickedness in life, God almighty, who created Heaven and earth, who is holy, pure, righteous, loving, compassionate, merciful, honest, wonderful is willing to allow you to come to Him as a child and build a relationship with Him even though you have done so many wrong things.

When we begin to understand what sin is we then can begin to understand just how deep the love of the Father is towards us. So many times I have sat and just been in awe of the Father's love for me and just how much compassion God has poured out on me because of my sins. I know in my heart I deserve to be in Hell but for some unknown reason I have found favor in the heart of God.

I also find it amazing just how many pastors and leaders I meet from all over treat me as if I have a disease or a deadly virus all because of my past but I realize that it is not right for me to judge people for their ignorance and stupidity.

As time goes by the more I realize just how much I have been forgiven by the Father and the more I want to know what is in the Father's heart. And one of the most amazing things I have learned is that even when a person is a coward or judgmental you must try to love them because ever since I have discovered just how much I am loved by the Father the more I seem to love people.

One of the most evil things I have ever seen in my life is how many Christians take someone for granted; most helpers are so burned out that they don't want to lift a finger because their leaders have taken advantage of them and taken them for granted.

But I wonder so many times why so many are in leadership? The church should set the trends but the church is now acting more like the world, so the world is telling the church what to do and how to act. I find it amazing how many leaders walk in fear, ignorance, defeat, self-righteousness and pride but because they have a college degree everyone seems to just accept them. But what happened to walking in love, power, authority, humility and kindness? College is great, getting an education is so wise but if getting intelligent causes you to become more like Satan why would you want that?

It's so sad how many will be in a lake of fire screaming and claiming how they have graduated from this or that college but yet have no deep concept of the love of the Father. So many that claim how their ministry makes millions and how much they are known worldwide will end up in Hell because instead of loving the Father and sharing truth, they love their mansions, their boats, their cars and getting praises from people from all over just like the Pharisees, they are so in love with the things of this world that they have for-gotten that the Father called them to be in love with Him and seek His heart but instead these people seek and love the things of this world.

I have discovered that so many have been abused and used by a person claiming to be a Christian that so many don't realize that the hour of giving an account is fast approaching and you will stand before the Father and have to explain why you needed to hurt, lie, deceive, steal, use, be a phony, be so self-righteous, walk in judg-ment, mock those that are poor and in need.

Yes my friends, the hour is fast approaching to give an account for your life, are you ready? So please come to the Father and repent of your sins and just allow the love of God to consume you.

CHAPTER 27

Well about a month later, Pastor Harley and I were cleaning up the construction from the new church being built but it was odd, I felt a very strong presence of something very evil but I didn't know what to do. Then all of a sudden Pastor Harley walked over to me and said, "Did you see it? The shadow moved". I knew right then and there that my pastor, Pastor Harley, was the real thing. Well, all of a sudden we both heard this evil growl and it said as clear as day, "This land is inhabited by the crow, the land of evil".

Pastor Harley said, "So it isn't inhabited by one demon, it's inhabited by several demons". All of a sudden Pastor Harley said, "Rick, how do you have victory over demonic powers?" I thought for a second and I realized that I wasn't sure. Then Pastor Harley said, "Take heed to what I am saying, these demons that are present are very bold and very powerful so they are not playing, so let's get on our knees. The first thing is walk in humility, now let's pray", so Pastor Harley began to speak to the giants and claimed just how awesome Jesus Christ is and how wonderful Jesus Christ is and then he said, "In Jesus Christ's name I come against all principalities, powers, authorities and all evil in Jesus Christ's name and I bind you up and send you back to where you came from", just then a big bang slammed the floor and it sounded just like thunder and said, "May we go into that retired rodeo bull across the street in that fenced lot?" And Pastor Harley said, "Go!" It was like a charge of horses running over the floor. I almost peed my pants because I could feel the intenseness of it all.

Pastor Harley said, "Ok, we have got work to do" and I said, "Aren't you marveled at what you just did, that was so intense and scary?" But Pastor Harley wasn't moved at all by it, he said, "Don't marvel that demons fear you, marvel that God almighty said Rick would you come to get to know me". Then I saw Pastor Harley start to cry as he was walking away and he said, "Oh don't be thrilled that demons fear you, be thrilled that you are called to walk with Jesus Christ".

Then Pastor Harley said, "There's so much power in your testimony, in the Blood, in Jesus Christ's name and in humility and keep that deep in your spirit". Then as Pastor Harley was walking away I was so marveled, I saw two warrior angels just hanging out with him and he was praising God, these two angels were dancing and it was one of the coolest things I have ever seen.

Well about four hours later the assistant pastor said, "Well we need to get ready because another place has just opened up to teach Yoga. And to make matters worse a very well-known speaker on that New Age garbage is advertising that he is going to be putting on a conference; so if you need to quit smoking, quit addictions, or lose weight, or just discover that inner self be ready because I am about to hypnotize over three thousand people to find freedom. But what so many people don't understand is that several people will have opened a portal over their own lives and so many will have opened their 3rd eye, so do I hear war?" Pastor Harley said, "Yes my friend, the war in the heavens is getting intense and there is a shaking in the spirit".

I was so marveled to hear these men talk about it. I knew there was a mighty shaking taking place because so many casual Christians I knew either are on fire for the things of God or they have fallen away completely. I really wonder how many people ever stop to just thank Jesus Christ for just being so great or so awesome. I remember reading in the word of God where Jesus healed 10 lepers but only one came back to thank him. I wonder how many times have I done this or how many times do people I know do this?

Well as I was picking up boards and scrap wood from outside, Pastor Harley had the word playing on CD so everyone working could hear the word of God. It's pretty awesome listening to the word of God on CD because it just seems so powerful just to listen to. But I couldn't stop thinking about the portals that my pastors were talking about.

CHAPTER 28

Then I saw my assistant pastor and I said, "Pastor, I don't remember your name, but the portals you were talking about can you explain this better to me?"

He then looked and me and said, "Rick I am Pastor Dean, yes portals are open doorways from a demon giving direct contact to a person. This is why a person would chew another person's face off, rape and eat another person, or why men have been known to rape a woman then sink his teeth into her chin or one of her breasts. Or why a woman just decides to cheat on her husband or leave her family, or kill her own children. Or why a person would want to harm a police officer for no apparent reason. See, so many don't realize that the enemy is like a roaring lion seeking to destroy everyone and anything he can.

See this is how portals can be opened; if you chant, listen to music that glorifies Lucifer or Satan by name, drugs, getting drunk, by being into white or black magic, being into Yoga, trying to contact a spirit through an Ouija board, playing with an Ouija board, Tarot cards, séances, crystal ball, palm or body reading, attending an Indian pow-wow, any type of sexual sin from whether you agree to it or not, having any items in your home that are of the occult, Hypnosis, witchcraft, voodoo, Satanism, trying to contact a spirit through water wishing or mirror glazing, calling on a spirit, contacting a medium or psychic, casting spells, using any type of wizard spells, music that glorifies a demon by name, asking a witch to cast a spell, Martial Arts, or worshiping a demon, animal or spirit by name. Self-mutilation, like cutting yourself, star gazing, wishing upon a star, or channeling"

Well as Pastor Dean was explaining this to me I was just amazed that so many don't even realize that there is great danger in opening yourself to a demon or spirit.

Then Pastor Dean said, "Just watch after that hypnosis confer- ence, crime will go up and so many will claim that they don't know why they are so depressed. Then while all this is going on our society will make all kinds of excuses as to why this or that is happening because they don't realize demons are speaking and because so very few understand this most people just assume that their thoughts were theirs but most thoughts people have are from demons or just a demon, if you have thoughts of committing a crime, hurting someone, raping someone, committing murder, or doing something evil or bizarre.

But most people don't comprehend intense warfare so if they get an evil or wicked thought they just assume it was from God so they just do it and then they blame God because they were so ignorant or prideful to stop and ask is this thought from God or Satan. See everything God speaks, Rick, will line up with the word of God and if you aren't sure go and ask a spirit filled pastor.

Also, Rick, so many think if I just was smart enough or had more money then I would go to church. See, God is not impressed how smart you are or how much money you have, what really touches God's heart is when you say Lord Jesus Christ, I humble myself, forgive me for my sins, now please come into my heart and teach me how to walk with You and teach me Your ways and decrees.

See Rick, when God hears this this moves God's heart in mighty ways. We will never be able to comprehend the mercy, compassion, kindness, love and God's grace but I will tell you this, Rick, nothing compares to the love of God".

Well as the months went by I really started to understand that walking in the power and authority in Christ isn't for my glory, it's for the glory of Christ.

Plus I now understand why Pastor Harley points out that if you are a true leader you should be sending people out to do warfare but if you can't trust them to do warfare for you or your church you should ask yourself what am I doing wrong?

Well after several years with Pastor Harley I realized it was time for me to be an evangelist and just travel around telling people about Jesus Christ. But as time goes by I will always keep Pastor Harley close to my heart

CHAPTER 29

W ell, after being on the road for about 18 months I got hold of Pastor Harley and he said, "You need to hear this", so I said, "Ok".

Pastor Harley went on to explain that they were doing an open testimony night and you could come and hear testimonies. And he said, "Rick, this little woman by the name of Tina gave a testimony that shook me on the inside and made every ounce of me to want to just cry and for two hours I cried and everyone was crying".

Pastor Harley said, "As Tina went forward and gave her testimony I was wondering why she was already crying, and this is what she said;

Tina said, "I gave birth to this bright and blond haired little girl, she was almost 8 ibs but so adorable. I looked in her eyes and she was just so cute and then her daddy came into the room and held our precious little Angel, we named her Angel Lee. Well our little one grew more and more through the years and she was daddy's little girl.

My husband's mom loved Angel so much, she just wanted to give her the world. My husband's mom's name was Mary. Mary was like a mom to me. Life seemed perfect in so many ways for several years. Then one night a drunk driver hit us head on and killed Angel Lee, I felt like I was going insane because I wanted to kill this drunk driver and my husband's rage was so bad, he talked about killing the drunk drivers own kids.

Well one day, about a month after the funeral, Grandma Mary came over and said, "As I was praying for Angel Lee she appeared before me and said thank you Grandma for the surprise you left me in your dresser, yes I love the locket you bought me and please tell my mommy and daddy I am doing great".

Then pastor Harley said Tina dropped a bomb on every ones heart and she said, "I told Mary, whom I love as a mom, that Angel Lee is gone and what she saw was a demon tugging on her emotions. Then she said Mary stood up and yelled at her and said I never told you or my son or Angel Lee about the locket so how else would you explain this? Tina you are wrong, Angel Lee said I can see her any time I want to and I can now spend hours with her. Well my husband heard his mom yell at me and when his mom told him what's going on he was all excited that his mom was able to see and hear Angel Lee every day. So as I tried to explain what familiar spirits are, my husband said I was the evil one and he told his mom I am moving in with you because if you can see Angel Lee daily I want to be in your house".

Well Pastor Harley said, "This is the part, Rick, that crushed me, he said Tina just got home from work about three weeks after her husband left her and had a knock on the door, it was divorce papers from her husband. So she called him right away and, according to their dead daughter, Angel Lee said mommy doesn't want to talk to me or see me so find someone else, daddy. So I just signed the papers and we were divorced within four months.

Then about two months after we were divorced I got a call from a police officer and he said I need you to help identify two bodies, I thought who do I know that died? Well I was at the morgue and the police officer opened up what looked like a refrigerator door and there was Mary, my ex-mother-in-law, all I could do was cry and ask why. Then the police officer opened up another refrigerator door and when he pulled back a sheet there was my ex-husband. I just stood there crying and asking God "Why? Why did two people I love so dearly have to die?"

Then the police officer said, according to what we can try to understand, your ex-husband left a note saying Angel Lee told your ex-husband to kill his mom so Mary will be up in heaven with Angel Lee and then, according to the suicide note, Angel Lee told your ex to kill himself so he will be with his mom and her up in heaven.

The police officer just held me in his arms and said, "I know this is so sad and horrible but they are not the first to be destroyed like this, I have met several mediums, psychics and others that left suicide notes claiming a past relative said to take their life so they did. It does sound strange but it's sad how many think it is ok to mess around with spirits thinking that it is ok till they turn on you".

Well I told Pastor Harley that story that Tina shared literally broke my heart and crushed me. Pastor Harley said, "Rick, she is a lot like you so we have decided to take her under our wing and see what she wants to accomplish in life and help her make it. We even asked her to move into our home because me and the misses just love her". So Pastor Harley let me know that Tina moved into their house.

Well I told Pastor Harley, "I was deeply surprised how many pastors and leaders are so afraid of offending people". And I said, "So many people are offended if you put up a rainbow because it's what the gay community like. So many are afraid to tell people what bible they preach out of because so many are offended if you don't preach out of the bible that they claim is right.

So many are offended if you are proud of your race or the color of your skin. So many are offended if you go to this or that store for groceries because the owner or company believe this or that. So many are afraid of offending the gay community. So many are offended by Mormons. Or offending Jehovah witnesses, so many are afraid of offending Catholics so they don't point out praying to Mary is wrong.

So many are afraid about talking about faith or the power of God, worried that they might offend someone who is a strong believer in Christian psychology or humanism. So many are afraid to speak up against abortion claiming it offends too many.

So many won't talk about spiritual warfare because they don't want to offend those that don't believe in warfare and so many now won't talk or preach about Hell because they don't want to be called judgmental.

Well some of you might consider me judgmental but I would rather offend you than my God who is living and powerful. So I make it clear that I will speak about Hell, spiritual warfare, sin, the Blood of the Lamb, Jesus being the Son of God, and the cross. I have to tell people from all over it is time that we quit worrying about offending people and we start being concerned about offending God, Jesus Christ or the Holy Spirit.

When I was in Houston I told a group at a church that it's time to grow up. Then I told Pastor Harley, "It's sad that so many Christians think I will just be a part of Yoga to learn to have peace, or I will just go to my deep mediation classes to find inner strength, or I will just call a psychic hotline when I need advice about money or my marriage.

"I find it so sad, Pastor Harley, just how many Christians walk the fence and then wonder why am I not being blessed, why do I feel God is so far away, or how come I don't feel close to God's heart? It is so interesting, Pastor Harley that people just don't get it". And Pastor Harley said, "Just continue to plant seeds and share the gospel worldwide and don't try to make anyone see the truth just plant seeds and allow the spirit of God to do the rest".

Well after almost a two hour wonderful talk with Pastor Harley he said he had to go.

So I am off to London now. I can't wait to see Pastor Harley again. There's just times in our lives that we want time to stand still because we feel loved and accepted but in a world that believes there's no hope and no one cares, it's so important to tell everyone about Jesus Christ the son of the most high God. Amen

CHAPTER 30

Well when I was in London things were going great but I was having some horrible dreams about the time I was in a mental ward. It was odd but for some reason I couldn't get the thoughts out of my mind so I decided to take a break from the ministry for a short time.

It was so nice to go back and see Pastor Harley and see what he was up to. Well he let me know he became a paranormal expert that deals with Demonic haunting so I decided to just be his shadow for a while and deal with this. Well pretty soon I was amazed how we were going all over pushing back the enemy and literally binding up spirits that were trying to destroy homes, businesses and families.

So as we were traveling I said, "Pastor Harley, help me please, I don't know what happened but it was like a very dark and powerful spirit of oppression that has come into my life and I just can't seem to get rid of it and I am having nightmares now". Well Pastor Harley said, "You have got more than one issue here, so let's deal with one at a time".

He said, "When oppression comes in like a flood that's when you need to find a way to be able to just be still and listen to worship music, don't do anything just listen. Then when you have finally got your eyes refocused back on Jesus and not the problem or problems now pray in the spirit. Many will come against this but who cares it's not them in a battle it's you, so who cares what someone else thinks.

Now plead the Blood over your mind and ask the Holy Spirit to cleanse your mind". Wow, immediately I was beginning to feel better being around Pastor Harley. I told Pastor Harley I feel better I said, "I just couldn't understand it, I went into an old house, it was so beautiful but this might sound strange but I heard the walls were whispering just like when I was in the mental ward, things seemed very confusing and hard to understand because it was like three people were talking all at one time so I went in the bathroom to pray alone and all of a sudden I heard whispering and giggling. Then I felt a cold chill. But I have never felt like this before so I came out of the bathroom and I talked with the pastor and home owners who asked me to come over there for lunch. And I said, "So how old are your little ones?" The home owners said, 'Well aren't you a strange one asking us about our children".

Then the Pastor said, "Rick are you ok?" Then I felt like I was losing my mind so the home owners said go lie down in our spare bedroom, you will be fine, you are just probably tired. Well when I lay my head down I literally heard, "Look in my eyes, don't you want me, I feel your pain". Then I heard crying so I sat up and it was like someone was just standing over me so I walked over to the window and I could hear crying again in the walls. Then as I began to walk closer to the door to leave a picture fell off the wall and shattered.

The home owners and pastor ran in to check on me and then the man said, "Why did you break that picture?" And the Pastor said, "Mark and Jane, I am so sorry I didn't realize this man who claimed to be a man of God would be like this" So they said, "You need to leave". So I grabbed my light jacket and as I started down the hallway I noticed a bedroom door was open so I glanced inside and saw a chair that looked just like the kind of chairs they would strap people in at the mental wards or insane asylums. Mark saw me glance at it and said, "Rick, that chair we picked up at an auction in Dallas, Texas at an auction, I guess a man choked to death in a cruel way while being restrained in this chair in an insane asylum. But as strange as it sounds ever since we brought the chair in our home things just haven't been the same".

Well the pastor called me a cab and I left but when I looked up in the upstairs window where I was there was a little girl in a dress, it looked like from the 1950s, it spooked me. Well Pastor Harley said, "Listen, so many psychics and mediums are running ads claiming how they can calm the spirits down, plus so many paranormal teams are running ads saying that they can investigate your home, so many people are turning to Catholics and mediums but let's literally clean the house or business out of all demonic activities or hauntings." Well the more time I spent with Pastor Harley the more I realized I had found my calling. I was breaking all kinds of demonic powers and authorities off of furniture, clothing, antiques, property. Wherever I went people just kept saying, "Wow, you really do bless the property" and I let people know it wasn't' me, it's the power and love of Jesus Christ.

Well I quit traveling and I realized so many need to hear the gospel right here in America. It saddened me how many Christians really don't know the power and authority they truly have in Jesus Christ's name.

I find it so amazing how many are so excited because they experience a demon, hear a voice, see a demonic vision or experience a spirit touching them. If people truly only understood just how much power they have in Christ.

Well it is time to run to the battle.

I hope you enjoyed my story!

PRAYERS

In the name of Jesus Christ, I bind up these spirits and all spirits related to these areas. All spirits of poverty, lack, anger, depression, pride, lust, destruction, shame, disgrace, rage, perversion, bestiality, religion, unbelief, doubt, despair, suicide, control, wickedness, envy, confusion, anxiety, fear, greed, selfishness, rejection, mental illnesses, bondage, cruelty, divination, sorcery, witchcraft, spells, homosexuality, hatred, discord, jealousy, sickness, rape, incest, unforgiveness, New Age, Satanism, occultism, murder, failure, torment, idolatry, hopelessness, frustration, foolishness, wickedness, revenge, addiction, mocking, callousness, twisting of the truth, seduction, worry, arguing, strife, suffering, illnesses, oppression, violence, manipulation, control.

Now I loose the spirit of truth, knowledge, long suffering, kindness, love, peace, joy, faithfulness, goodness, forgiveness, mercy, grace, gentleness, self-control, compassion, tongues, mercy, grace, gentleness, self-control, compassion, tongues of fire, wisdom, hope, restoration, healing, intelligence, power, self-discipline, humility, creativity, loyalty, riches, honor, strength, favor, blessing, wealth, riches, prosperity, and above all, the fear of the Lord. AMEN!

PRAYER FOR THE NATION

Please forgive this nation for killing unborn children, for seeking the paranormal and not You. Please forgive us for getting into many wicked and perverted sexual sins. Please forgive us for looking at animals as sexual objects. Please forgive us for raping women and abusing children. Please forgive us for killing children and harming children. Please forgive this nation for turning men and woman into sex slaves. Please forgive us for throwing teenagers out on the streets as if they're trash. Please forgive us for the prostitution that is running ramped in this country.

Please loving Father, forgive us for all the ruthless and senseless killings in this country. Please forgive us for our greed and selfishness. Please forgive us for promoting violence in movies and music. Please forgive us for promoting perversion and wickedness in our music and in our movies. Please forgive us for promoting so much bestiality in movies, please forgive us for all the lust we have in our hearts. Please forgive us for not fearing You. Forgive us please for doubting You. Please forgive us for the pride we carry in our hearts. Please forgive us for the pride we have in our ministries, in our cars, in our homes, in our businesses. Please forgive us for seeking out success, power, and wealth, when all You want us to do is seek a friendship with You. Please forgive us for seeking more education and more knowledge, when we should seek You first.

Please forgive us for taking man's wisdom over Your word. Forgive us please for putting our trust in psychology over what You say. Please forgive us for seeking out Satanism, Sorcery, Magic, Mediums, Psychics, New Age, Wicca, Eastern Religions, foreign gods. Please forgive us for getting in to Erotic Asphyxiation, Sadomasochism. Please forgive us for Necrophilia. Please forgive us for wanting to speak to the dead. Please forgive us for necromancy. Please forgive us for all of our debauchery. Please forgive us for wanting to know our horoscopes. Please forgive us for allowing someone to put us under hypnosis. Please forgive us for going to a séances, listening to Tarot card readers. Please forgive us for calling white magic good. Please forgive us for glorifying the things of Satan and his demons. Please forgive us for worshiping angels. Please forgive us for putting faith in good luck charms. Please forgive us for being self-seeking. Please forgive us for our arrogance. Please forgive us for all the porn made in this country. Please forgive us for leaving our spouses because someone is younger looking.

Please forgive us for grieving your Holy Spirit. Please forgive us for compromising. Please forgive us for not spending time with You. Please forgive us for taking Your word and You for granted. Please forgive us for the hardness of our hearts to where we mock and ridicule others especially because of their faith in You. Please forgive us the wickedness in our prayers when actually we are speaking curses. Please forgive us for trying to fill that void that is in our hearts that You put in there so we would have a relationship with You. Please forgive us for turning our lives over to sex, drugs, alcohol, gambling, porn, wealth, greed, education, knowledge, power, when we should turn our lives and hearts over to You.

God the Most High God, please, please forgive us for these sins, we are a sinful nation and we need our forgiveness in this very hour. Please come dear Lord, come and bring Your glory.

Amen

PRAYER FOR HELP

In Jesus Christ's name I bind up these spirits and all spirits connected to them. Spirits of poverty, lack, anger, bestiality, depression, pride, lust, destruction, shame, disgrace, rage, perversion, religion, unbelief, doubt, despair, suicide, control, wickedness, envy, confusion, anxiety, fear, greed, selfishness, Rejection, mental illnesses, bondage, cruelty, divination, sorcery, witchcraft, spells, homosexuality, hatred, discord, jealousy, sickness, rape, incest, unforgiveness, new age, Satanism, occults, murder, failing, torment, idolatry, hopelessness, frustration, foolishness, wickedness, revenge, addictions, mocking, calloused, twisting the truth, seductive, worry, arguing, strife, suffering, illnesses, oppression, violence, seducing, manipulation

Now I loose the spirit of truth, knowledge, longsuffering, kindness, love, peace, joy, faithfulness, goodness, forgiveness, mercy, grace, gentleness, self-control, compassion, tongues of fire, wisdom, hope, restoration, healing, intelligence, power, self-discipline, humility, creativity, loyalty, riches, honor, strength, great favor, blessings, wealth, riches, prosperity, and above all the fear of the Lord

Father in Heaven forgive me for walking in judgment towards others, I have been more concerned about someone smoking cigarettes or smelling like cigarettes than I have been about showing the love of Jesus Christ. I have been acting like the Pharisees; it's not a matter of what goes in a body but what is in the heart of man. I should be more concerned about walking in the power, love, gentleness, authority and compassion of You, Father, than be concerned about a person smoking.

Father in Heaven, please forgive me for being legalistic and judging companies that promote lingerie, who am I to judge a person or a company? There is not one scripture in the bible that says lingerie is evil but yet I stand in judgment because I don't like that clothing, but when did I become so powerful and so self-righteous that I could speak against something. If I don't like something I should be praying for it and not cursing it.

Father in Heaven, please forgive me for standing in judgment and mocking Christian rock music, please forgive me for speaking against another child of yours anointing, who am I to claim what is or isn't from you? If you called one man to scream or talk softly in music it is none of my business and you didn't ask me for my opinion.

FREEDOM FROM CURSES

Now that we realize there are curses, we need to realize why there are curses and what the effects of curses are.

#1 Reason for a curse is not listening to what God says; when God speaks we need to listen. If you want the blessings of God do what He says to do.

#2 So many people say, well, I don't know what God is saying, if you're a spirit filled Christian you should be able to determine what God is wanting or asking you to do. See, sometimes we get off track but when we do God is quick to help us if we walk in humility and love.

If God is so powerful to create the world and us, do we really believe that he would keep his will for our lives a secret? Each child of God, God has a plan and a purpose for our lives. God almighty loves us so much that He wants us to be filled with joy and peace but we must humble ourselves and seek His face to find out what it is that He's calling us to do. Many times what we want is what God has put in our hearts to do in life for His glory not ours.

Now read this carefully: By being obedient to God here's the list of blessings listed in Deuteronomy, Chapter 28. As you read this list please think about these blessings.

1. Exaltation
2. Reproductive
3. Health
4. Prosperity
5. Victory
6. That we are the head and not the tail
7. That we will be above and not beneath.

Now that we can see clearly what the blessings are let's now look at the curses.

A. Humiliation
B. Barrenness
C. Sickness and disease of every kind
D. Poverty, failure, lack
E. Defeat in every area of life.
F. We will be the tail and not the head
G. We will be below and not above
H. Confusion

Indications of Curses:

(1) Mental, emotional, financial and spiritual breakdown
(2) Repeated sickness or diseases, especially hereditary sickness.
(3) Feminine problems - barrenness, miscarriage, menstruation problems or uncommon bleeding.
(4) Breakdown of marriage, breakdown in relationships, siblings fighting as adults, family alienation, and lack of mercy or love between children.
(5) Financial insufficiency, poverty, lack, car accidents repeated, loss of jobs over and over again, or getting hurt on the job at several different jobs, Accident prone.
(6) People dying at early ages or unexplained deaths.

There are also generational curses.

I have seen a location be under a curse to where no matter what the business is it either went under or evil things have happened at this location. It's very sad but this one place that was just a small bar off the highway had more deaths and rapes than big bars or night clubs. When a place has had a violent, evil or wicked crime committed on its land that land must be prayed over or that location belongs to demonic powers.

One time a man bought a car that a person had committed suicide in and after he took ownership of that car he then felt suicidal thoughts and he finally came to a point where he got rid of the car, then all the thoughts of suicide left him.

We need to realize we live in a nonstop spiritual war. Now here are some reasons that we come under a curse.

A. Having false gods, are you putting your trust in an Ouija board, Tarot cards, dreams, crystals, good luck charms, sex, alcohol, drugs, gambling, séances, wizards, dream catchers, horoscopes, or mediums or witches? If you are then you have put a curse on yourself and your family because God the creator of heaven and earth must be on the throne at all times. How can we say we love God but we don't trust him? (Exodus 20: 3& 4, Deuteronomy 27: 15)

B. Disrespect for parents, so many young people these days are killing and harming their parents and then wonder why they are being locked up for many years. Young people I realize that life isn't easy but remember if you commit a crime you eventually will do the time. So many young people will never have a family and will never experience the joys of life because they are sitting behind bars just waiting for their life to end because every day that they wake up they will sit behind prison or mental ward walls. (Deuteronomy 27: 16)

C. Treachery against a neighbor, who is your neighbour? A friend, a church member, a co-worker, see, we must represent Christ at all times. Anyone that comes to you is your neighbor. Deuteronomy 27: 17)

D. Injustice to the weak, if you study your word you will find throughout scriptures that God has a heart for those that are poor and those that are fatherless. (Deuteronomy 27: 18 & 19)

E. Illicit sex Deuteronomy 27: 20-23, and Revelation 9:21 "And they did not repent of their murders or their sorcerers or their sexual immorality or their thefts". See, if you have sex with an animal, or person outside of a man and woman marriage, you are in sin. So many times people think that I only had oral sex with this person or with this animal so that can't be wrong but in the eyes of God it is wrong.

Now here is a list of why so many fall under a curse:

Stealing, lying, being cruel to animals or children, having no mercy, showing lack of love or compassion, self-seeking or self-centered, prideful, boastful, angry, easily angered, murder, rape,

incest, doing evil against God's anointed, harming or being destructive towards your neighbor's things or harming or being destructive
towards the house of God, harming or being destructive towards a
poor person, speaking evil against someone that is seeking after the
heart of God, name calling, names to a person that is a Christian,
being self-righteous, husbands not forgiving their wives, husbands
not honoring and respecting their wives with their words and actions,
husbands that treat their wives poorly, husbands that compare their
wife's body to what they saw in a porn magazine or movie, husbands that look at porn or get into calling 1-800 # to talk to another
woman in a lustful conversation, Wives that dishonor their husbands
because they are speaking evil about them. Wives that withhold
sexual gratification from their husbands because he doesn't make
enough money for you to be happy, or buy you enough things. Men
that treat their wives like a sex toy.

BREAKING UNGODLY SOUL TIES

Two more reasons for a curse to come upon you:

A. Objects in homes (Deuteronomy 7: 26) We are to have
   no abominable things in our home. Years ago I was given
   a beautiful necklace and it had a nice stone with it. Well I
   went to go get it cleaned and the jeweller who I knew was
   a Christian said, "Tim, you have got to see this", well he
   showed me the nice stone under a magnifying glass and it
   was a Buddha Temple inside the stone. Well we destroyed
   both the necklace and the stone because anything connected
   to Buddha, which is a false god, a Christian should have
   nothing to do with.

Then also years ago a woman came to me and said my children
suffer from severe nightmares but my husband and I don't know

147

why. Well I knew this couple were Christians and they stood against Disney so I could not think of what would cause their children to have nightmares. So I went over to their house and someone had given this little child of theirs Pokemon cards, so I explained to them that Pokemon means "monster in your pocket", so I asked the little one, do you want your nightmares to go away? Well he said yes, so I said can we burn all these cards? And he said yes, so we did and that little boy no longer had nightmares. See Satan will not knock on your door asking to come in, he will find a way to destroy you and your family if he can.

B. Soul ties; these are soul ties which are contrary to God's purposes, In adultery, fornication (especially past sexual relationships). Ungodly soul ties can bring spiritual sickness. I tell people anything related to that past ungodly soul tie relationship needs to be destroyed, stuffed animals, jewellery, clothes, etc, anything that causes you to look back like Lot's wife did before she became a pillar of salt because she looked back at Sodom and Gomorrah before God destroyed it.

1 Corinthians 6: 18: Flee sexual immorality. "Every sin that a man does is outside the body, but he who commits sexual immorality sins against his own body". See, oaths are not of God but many people have cut themselves and taken an oath, we need to repent from all oaths and ungodly soul ties. My graduating class was so evil and self-centered that I have decided not to have any contact with my old classmates because hardly any of them see any of the wrongs that we did. Can light fellowship with darkness?'

Ok, it's time to break these curses, so let's look at these scriptures closely:

1 John 3:8 "He who sins is of the devil, for the devil has sinned from the beginning. For this purpose the Son of God was manifested, that He might destroy the works of the devil.

Isaiah 10:27 "It shall come to pass in that day That his burden will be taken away from your shoulder, And his yoke from your neck, And the yoke will be destroyed because of the anointing oil. We must repent from all sin".

A. We must renounce in the name of Jesus Christ, all demonic activity and sinful activity of our past and/or our parent's or grandparent's past. We must repent and ask God to forgive and sever all demonic curses, soul ties, and actions related to that curse.

B. We must resist the evil one and submit under God. James 4: 7:" Therefore submit to God. Resist the devil and he will flee from you". The devil is a liar, so if he says you're going to be worthless just like your mom was or your dad was tell him you're a liar. Just because your aunt and mom were prostitutes doesn't mean you have to be. Or just because your father is in prison doesn't mean you have to go there as well.

C. Now meditate on the word of God; believe it, memorize it, stand on it and confess what you want God to do in your life by speaking out scriptures. God loves you and He truly does have a plan and a purpose for your life so please draw close to Him and He will draw close to you.

Now here are just a few examples of how to break curses:
In Jesus Christ's name, I ask you Heavenly Father to forgive my grandfather for being a mason and I ask that all demonic curses and oaths that were spoken out will be broken as of right now in the name of Jesus Christ and through the blood of Christ I have been

149

redeemed from all demonic curses and powers. So as of this second I am now free in Christ.

If your parents called you names here's one just for you;

In the name of Jesus Christ I am free from all demonic and evil word curses that my parents spoke over me because according to the word of God I am more than a conquer through Christ Jesus, So now I sever all demonic curses spoken over me and I plead the blood of Christ over me spiritually, mentally, financially, emotionally and my whole being.

If you give God more of your time, love and energy you will find out none of it was in vain. God will reward those that seek His face.

I don't know if anyone has heard of the movie (Facing The Giants) but I would like to strongly recommend that you watch this movie because it will change your life, because it has brought many blessings to me.

So many don't realize that Jesus Christ not only wants to help you discover your destiny but help you to reach your destiny in life. So many people have got so many wrong concepts about Jesus Christ because so many people have been hurt by them, abused them, tore them down, and betrayed them. But I am here to tell you no matter what sin or wrong you have done in life God wants to forgive you.

John 3:16 "for God so loved the world that He gave His only begotten Son, that whoever believes in Him should not perish but have everlasting life".

So please cry out to Jesus Christ right now and just say "Jesus, forgive me for my sins and come inside of me and be my Lord and Savior. Teach me Your ways and Your concepts and Your decrees. Now I ask this in Jesus Christ's Holy name. Amen.

Father in Heaven, I ask that You will please forgive me for being sadistic towards animals, people or my spouse. I am so deeply sorry for being sexually aroused, by wanting to harm someone or something. Please Father, by your mercy and grace, I ask that You will teach me how to love someone, animals or my spouse with a holy love and a genuine love.

Please Father in Heaven teach me how to be gentle hearted and teach me how to be pure, give me a heart of flesh.

Please Father in Heaven, uproot all the seeds of cruelty, wickedness, vengeance, and evil out of my heart and I humbly ask You, please will You give me a heart of mercy, compassion, grace, love, kindness and understanding.

Please Father forgive me for having a desire to want to kill myself or someone else. Give me Your heart and please teach me to be like Christ.

Father in Heaven, please forgive me for having sex with animals anal or oral, I know it is wrong so please wash my mind and my whole being in the blood of Jesus Christ. Father please take away the desires I have of wanting to have sex with animals and please give me a heart of purity and holiness. I am so sorry my Father for seeing animals as sex objects, wash my mind and teach me how to be pure and Holy, in Jesus Christ's name I ask these prayers and I seal these prayers in the blood of Jesus Christ. Amen.

Please Father in Heaven, forgive me for being sadistic and cruel to animals or people, even to children. I am so sorry that I have abused the power I have and the strength over people. Please Lord Jesus Christ teach me how to walk in humility, compassion and love. Forgive me Father for my ignorance, pride, selfishness and ego. Please come now Lord Jesus and help me become more like You, In Jesus Christ's name I pray. Amen

Father in Heaven please forgive me for being sexually attracted to animal furs, I am so sorry that I become sexually aroused when looking at dead animals or the furs of animals. Please uproot any sick and perverted sexual thoughts or ideas in me and uproot them. In Jesus Christ's name I ask You will help me become a man of God and I ask in Jesus Christ's name to give me a heart of purity, in Jesus Christ's name. Amen.

Father in Heaven please forgive me for masturbating to pictures of dead men or women and even animals. I am so deeply sorry that I become sexually aroused by pictures of dead men or women who have been killed in an accident or been beaten to death.

Please Father help me discover what is pure and Holy and give me desires that are from You that are pure and righteous.

Please Father in Heaven uproot the evil and wicked seeds planted in me and give me a heart of God. Lord Jesus Christ please give me the heart of Christ and please show me what Your desires are and teach me what it means to have healthy and normal sexual desires according to Your word. In Jesus Christ's name I ask that You cleanse my mind of all evil in Jesus' name. Amen.

Father in Heaven please forgive me for wanting to sexually touch several women that I have seen pictures of in the newspaper or on the news that have been beaten to death, took their own lives or have been killed in an accident.

I am so deeply sorry Father that I wanted to have sex with so many of these women or take one of their hands and masturbate with it. Father in heaven I need your help I have had so many evil and wicked desires please come and rescue me, I am consumed in thoughts of evil perversion and thoughts of sexual evil thoughts, help me, I am crying out loud, please. I surrender all to you, help me Lord Jesus.

In Jesus Christ's name I ask that my mind and whole entire being be washed and cleansed in the blood of the lamb. Amen. And now I seal these prayers in Jesus Christ name. Amen

Father in Heaven please forgive me for being a sex addict and looking at the opposite sex as a piece of meat. Please forgive me for not honoring and respecting others as my brothers and sisters in the Lord. Please forgive me for wanting to have sex hourly and thinking about having sex with everyone I meet and forgive me for lusting in my heart non-stop after so many. Please Loving Father give me the heart of Christ Jesus and teach me how to walk in purity and holiness. Please wash my mind of lust and give me pure and holy eyes in Jesus Christ's name I pray. Amen

Father in Heaven please forgive me for cutting myself, burning myself and harming myself. I am so deeply sorry for looking at myself and comparing myself to a maggot or a piece of trash. Lord Jesus You suffered for me and You were crucified for me, I am so sorry I have discovered no human value in myself and I am so sorry I have found no value of any part of me. I am so sorry that instead of turning to You for comfort I have turned to cutting and punishing myself for so many reasons. Please Lord Jesus restore my mind, my heart and my emotions and please Lord Jesus teach me how to walk hand in hand with you hourly, in Jesus Christ's name I pray. Amen.

CLOSING PORTALS

Several people have sent me messages or made comments, how do I close a portal? Please listen carefully, no matter what you have done repent, yes repentance is the first part of being set free. See God is looking for humility, look at this scripture, when we humble ourselves the power of God moves.

Acts 19:19 Also, many of those who had practiced magic brought their books together and burned them in the sight of all. And they counted up the value of them, and it totaled fifty thousand pieces of silver.

If you were given anything by the other person that you were in sin or unholy relationship with, such as rings, flowers, cards, bras, lingerie, sex toys, stuffed animals, whips, chains of any kind, Tarot cards, Ouija board, crystals, dream catcher, pictures, etc, I would strongly suggest you destroy them to where nobody can have them or would want them but if you can't destroy it bury it deep in the ground! Such things symbolize the ungodly relationship and can hold a soul tie in place.

I have met people who had a close grandma leave her Ouija board to her granddaughter and all of a sudden this woman's life was being destroyed because of the demonic power coming off of this board.

I have also met a young man who was left original pictures of several serial killers and he started developing mental problems. See, God wants to bless you, question is are you willing to humble yourself to be set free?

God has called you to walk in victory, joy and peace but so many want to try to either put a band aid on the situation or want to think there's another way so they turn to psychology, new age, medicine man, witchdoctor, a Catholic priest, some sort of eastern religion, but there's nothing that can set you totally free except the power of Jesus Christ, so please humble yourself today right now and just say "Lord Jesus Christ forgive me for my sins and cleanse me with Your blood please. I ask right now that You would sever all ties with demonic powers from them to me or me to them. In Jesus Christ's name I plead the blood over these prayers. Amen.

Father in Heaven forgive me for harming myself or hurting myself by trying Erotic asphyxiation. Please forgive me for strangling myself and not realizing my life isn't based on getting sexual fulfillment but my life is based on serving You. Please help me get sexual fulfillment by making love to my spouse and not through other means. In Jesus Christ's name I pray. Amen.

Father in Heaven please forgive me for putting objects up myself or in me to become sexually pleased. I am asking You to please help me to become sexually pleased by my spouse whom I am married to. Please give me a heart for my spouse and not a toy or object to help me get sexually off in Jesus Christ's name I pray. Amen

Father in Heaven please forgive me for holding onto my grandmother's rosary beads and anything else that I knew was from the enemy. I am so sorry I allowed my emotions to be over taken to where instead of standing up for the things of God, I allowed Satan to convince me that I needed to keep things because of sentimental value. Lord Jesus Christ forgive me please and please You be my Lord, not my emotions. Amen

Father in Heaven forgive me for keeping my grandparent's statues of Mary and of Jesus that came from a Catholic church. I am so sorry that my thoughts and emotions were more wrapped up in sentimental values instead of destroying something that I know was an idol and is just looked at as a piece of religion and nothing to do with a deep and meaningful relationship. So in Jesus Christ's name please forgive me and help me destroy all religious items.

Father in Heaven please forgive me for holding onto any of my grandfather's masonic items or holding onto any of my grandfather's or dads items that they got when they were in the war that have a Buddha or a Swastika on them. All items that have wicked and evil symbols on them need to be destroyed no matter how much they claim it is worth, it is still under a curse and in the eyes of God it is evil to have in your home. So please dear God forgive me for keeping these things and now give me the strength to bury them. Amen.

Father in Heaven please forgive me for trying to communicate with my dead dad, mom, sister, brother, grandparent, cousin, friend or any other person. I am so deeply sorry for trying to communicate with the dead thinking it was ok for me to do this. I am so sorry for trying to get advice from a dead relative, bible hero, or a dead world leader. God Almighty my trust and my desires should be in You and You only. Forgive me for trying to gain financial, spiritual or some wisdom from the dead by gaining insight from the other side. Father in heaven please help me to seek Your face, give me a desire and a heart to know you. In Jesus Chris's name I pray. Amen

Father in Heaven please forgive me for seeking wisdom, insight, my healing, prosperity or blessings by putting my trust in my Horoscope, yoga, séances, Tarot cards, Ouija board, psychic, medium, palm reading, body reading, star gazing, water wishing, tea leaves, voodoo, angel worship, demon worship, fire gazing, chanting, hypnosis, good luck charms, crystal ball, my pastor, my friend, my mom or my dad, auto writing, wearing certain clothes, throwing salt over my shoulder, crucifix or by holding a rosary. My God, My God forgive me for not humbling myself and putting my trust in the one and only true way to find answers to life and that is Jesus Christ. Please Lord Jesus Christ forgive me for being so stubborn and prideful by not seeking Your face and seeking the true heart of God. Lord Jesus Christ restore my life and help me stay on the right path walking with You, Lord Jesus Christ hourly. Amen.

Father in Heaven please forgive me for falling away from You and seeking after false gods. Forgive me please for allowing sin and the pleasures of sin to draw me away from You and not realizing I was falling into a deeper deception thinking the pleasures of sin would last forever but I was deceived and now I am hurting and lost. Please, Lord Jesus Christ I plead with You, restore me please to where I can feel the heart of God leading and guiding me into your truth and your ways. So in Jesus Christ's name give me a new hope and a deeper than before relationship with You Jesus, please, and help me restore my faith in You, in Jesus Christ's name I pray. Amen.

Father in Heaven forgive me for holding an offense towards those that have used me and have hurt me, God may You bless those that have cursed me, used me and have hurt me. Lord Jesus when they were crucifying you, You said, "Lord, forgive them for they know not what they are doing", so I ask you Jesus Christ give me a heart like Yours and give me a compassion to love people like You do. Lord Jesus Christ give me a heart to know the deep intimacy love of God and help me walk in the deepness of love daily towards people. Now I ask these prayers to be sealed in the blood of Christ. Amen.

Father in heaven I want to be deeper in a relationship with you, I want to know if I hurt You or offend You, so please I am crying out, Lord Jesus if there is anyone or anything in my life that puts a wall or a blockage from me being in a deeper relationship with You then please show me and give me the strength to remove it please. Lord Jesus my heart just breaks because I want to know You and I want to hear You. Please give me a deeper desire to want to know You and fall deeper in love with You. My life and heart are in Your hands, please draw me closer Lord Jesus Christ and let me experience so much more of You and let me feel Your presence. Lord Jesus be tangible, consume me in Your love, my Lord and Savior. Lord Jesus let me just be in awe of You daily. Breathe on me Jesus Christ to where I can feel it and shout for joy because I know it's You. Lord Jesus I want You, yes I want so much more of You. Consume me Lord Jesus Christ and I ask these prayers in Your awesome name in Jesus Christ. Amen.

Lord Jesus Christ please forgive me for not casting down thoughts and imaginations. Lord Jesus I know it is sinful to think about having sex with the same sex, please forgive me for entertaining thoughts of wanting to kiss someone of the same sex as me and forgive me for claiming its just for fun when I know Jesus Christ died on a cross because of sin, so sin must never be referred to as just for fun. Please Lord Jesus Christ forgive me for not taking heed to what Your word says. Please give me a heart of flesh and a heart that would take heed to Your word. In Jesus Christ name I pray. Amen.

Lord Jesus Christ forgive me for entertaining thoughts of suicide. I am deeply sorry Lord Jesus for not casting these thoughts and imaginations down. You created me for a purpose so it is not right that I would entertain evil thoughts when I know that You made me and Your only Begotten Son, Lord Jesus, died on a cross so there is hope even when I can't see it. Please Father in Heaven forgive me for listening to spirits telling me there is no hope and life is meaningless.

(Please if you are feeling suicidal contact a pastor right away or a professional please)

Father in Heaven please forgive me for believing in lies about love because love is not being controlled, called filthy names, love is not slapped, cussed at, spit on, punched, kicked, laughed at, made fun of, ridiculed, beat on, have your hair pulled out, being degraded, being made to feel worthless, being forced to have sex, being raped, being burned, being forced to sleep in a dog pen, being forced to sleep in a garage, being withheld food, sleep, clothes, being forced to surrender all your money or your worldly possessions, feeling threatened, being manipulated, being lied to, being used, being forced to eat dog or cat food, being cut, being knifed, burned, tortured, being forced to suffer, being forced to wear a dog chain or dog collar, being sodomized, being drugged, forced to lose weight, threatened, being forced to do anything that is mentally, emotionally, psychical or spiritual that is harmful to you or life threatening. Being forced to do anything that you feel is mentally, emotionally, spiritually or psychically wrong. Also love is not being a punching bag for anyone. Being told you need to lose weight or you need to change the clothes you wear, or the way you are, and love is not staying with a spouse that cheats on you with other women or men.

1 CORINTHIANS 13:4-7 tells us what love is,
4 Love suffers long and is kind; love does not envy; love does not parade itself, is not puffed up;
5. does not behave rudely, does not seek its own, is not provoked, thinks no evil;
6. does not rejoice in iniquity, but rejoices in the truth;

7 bears all things, believes all things, hopes all things, endures all things.

Father forgive me for not humbling myself and sexually satisfying my partner, I know in part it is my fault that they have fallen into sin because I didn't desire to have sex for so long I set up my spouse to fall. Please give me a heart to love my spouse sexually, mentally, emotionally and help me to find my spouse attractive even though they have gained weight. Father in Heaven forgive me for not being there to listen to their needs and their desires. I am so sorry I ignored my spouse when they needed to talk and just share their heart. I am so sorry dear God when my spouse needed just to have a shoulder to cry on or someone to just open up to or just a soft word of encouragement I wasn't there emotionally for them.

When my spouse needed to be honored and stood up for I allowed my family to tear my spouse down because I was a coward and was walking in fear of man. Please Lord Jesus forgive me for claiming to be a Christian but denying the power of God living in me by being a coward, I am deeply ashamed of myself and I ask you please Lord Jesus forgive me and help me become that person in You that will walk in the power and authority in Christ Jesus I pray now and seal these prayers in Your blood. Amen.

Father in Heaven please forgive me for denying Your power and walking in fear of man. I know You asked me to do this or that but Lord Jesus because of the fear of man or offending my parents, siblings or friends I didn't do what You really showed me what You wanted me to do because of fear and because I have been a coward. Please Lord Jesus give me a heart to know Your will and Your ways and now help me to walk in the power and authority in You Lord Jesus Christ.

Help me Lord Jesus Christ not to be a coward and walk in fear and rebellion. Lord Jesus forgive me, I am so deeply sorry for not being that powerful person in You and doing what I know I was called to do. So in Jesus Christ's name be strong where I am weak in Christ Jesus. Amen.

Father in Heaven I am so deeply sorry I claim to be a Christian and I claim to love You but I am doing what Jesus rebuked people for doing, he said, "Why do you call me Lord, Lord but not do what I tell you to do". Father I am so phony because I claim to love Jesus so much but I don't do any of the things He has told us to do, forgive me for worrying about offending someone and forgive me for being a coward.

Lord Jesus I know You are shaking the fence and I must decide whose side will I stand for, the power of God or the power of Satan, you didn't call me Lord Jesus to be lukewarm. How can I claim to love You, Lord Jesus but not do what You say to do?

Father in heaven help me to follow the words of Jesus Christ and help me become not just a hearer of the word of God but an actual doer of the word of God. Father in Heaven please don't have Your son puke me out of His mouth, give me a heart that will catch on fire for the things of God and help me to learn how to walk in the things of Jesus. In Jesus Christ's name I ask that my heart would be transformed to be like Jesus Christ. Amen

Father in Heaven please teach me how to walk in faithfulness, accountability, teachable, power, authority, humility and above all things love. Please give me a heart to want to give a dying world that is filled with sin that there is hope in Jesus Christ. Amen

MODEL PRAYER

In the name of Jesus Christ, I bind up these spirits and all spirits related to these areas. All spirits of poverty, lack, anger, depression, pride, lust, destruction, shame, disgrace, rage, perversion, bestiality, religion, unbelief, doubt, despair, suicide, control, wickedness, envy, confusion, anxiety, fear, greed, selfishness, rejection, mental illnesses, bondage, cruelty, divination, sorcery, witchcraft, spells, homosexuality, hatred, discord, jealousy, sickness, rape, incest, unforgiveness, New Age, Satanism, occultism, murder, failure, torment, idolatry, hopelessness, frustration, foolishness, wickedness, revenge, addiction, mocking, callousness, twisting of the truth, seduction, worry, arguing, strife, suffering, illnesses, oppression, violence, manipulation, control.

Now I loose the spirit of truth, knowledge, longsuffering, kindness, love, peace, joy, faithfulness, goodness, forgiveness, mercy, grace, gentleness, self-control, compassion, tongues, mercy, grace, gentleness, self-control, compassion, tongues of fire, wisdom, hope, restoration, healing, intelligence, power, self-discipline, humility, creativity, loyalty, riches, honor, strength, favor, blessing, wealth, riches, prosperity, and above all, the fear of the Lord. AMEN!

In Jesus Christ's name I come against principalities, against powers, against the rulers of the darkness of this age, against spiritual hosts of wickedness in the heavenly places, and I bind you up right now in Jesus Christ's name to where you cannot and will not operate at all. All your plans and all your tactics have been crushed now, I openly expose you to the light and from this day forward this house, room, business, property, land is now under the power and authority of the living Jesus Christ who is Lord and Savior of all, so by His blood this place has now been set free

Where there is freedom there is the Spirit of the most high God who raised Jesus Christ from the dead, so Praise Jesus Christ, it's time to get excited.

In Jesus Christ's name I come against the spirit or emotionalism, I refuse to allow my emotions to control me and be a god to me, Jesus Christ is my Lord and Savior and even though I may deeply desire to live near a friend or family member, or I may desire to keep this or that because it is an antique, like my dad giving me a porn magazine from the 60s, or my mom giving me a rosary from the 40s, no matter how much it is worth I will destroy it because no matter what it is or how much my heart longs for it I want nothing to come in between my relationship with Jesus Christ, so right now I demand my emotions and my heart's desires to come under submission of the power of God and I want the heart of God in me, so in Jesus Christ's name, I declare Jesus Christ is Lord over my emotions and wants, in Christ Jesus I pray. Amen

In Jesus Christ's name I come against the spirit of lack and poverty, you have no right being in my life, my spouse's life or my child's life, I come against you, not in my name or in the power I have but in the name of Jesus Christ and in the power and authority of Jesus Christ's name I come against you. I break your power and I crush your power in Jesus Christ's name and I now release the anointing of God to bless me with every blessing and needs I have and I ask that if any demon that tries to stop the flow of my blessings and prosperity will be severely punished and sent back where it came from. In Jesus Christ's name I ask these things. In Jesus Christ's name seal in the anointing, power, authority and power in Christ's name. Amen.

In Jesus Christ's name I come against the spirit of mental illness and I declare from this day forward that the spirit of fear will not cause mental illness in me, my spouse or child anymore, for God Almighty has not given me or my spouse or my child a spirit of fear but of power love and a (sound mind) since so many mental illnesses come from fear, and so many take their life because they fear this or that I come against this spirit and I declare that wherever I go I pray that peace, power, authority, love and a sound mind will be released through the power of the Holy Spirit living in me, now I speak these things out and ask Jesus Christ to anoint and bless my prayers in Jesus Christ's name and sealed in the name of Jesus Christ, covered in the Blood. Amen.

In Jesus Christ's name, right now I declare that no word, nor weapon formed, planned and spoken against me shall prosper in any way shape or form. I declare that Jesus Christ's name is above every name and above every curse so whatever anyone says or thinks of me I cast all things down under the blood of Jesus Christ's name and I pray right now that my shield of faith is mighty and stopping the arrows from the enemy. I pray that Jesus, yes Jesus Christ my friend, my Savior, my Lord and Light will protect me and lead me into a deeper walk with Him and the loving Holy Spirit will lead me and guide me into all truth and the knowledge and wisdom of truth Amen. I pray in Jesus Christ's name. Amen.

In Jesus Christ's name I bind up the spirit of Adramelech which deceives women into believing that having sex with animals would be ok and sexually satisfying. I bind up this spirit and all perverted spirits with it and I send you back to where you came from, you no longer will hold any power or authority in my neighborhood or city in Jesus Christ's name I prayer. Amen. And I ask Lord Jesus Christ that You will protect me from all demonic powers. In Jesus Christ's name. Amen

In Jesus Christ's name, I ask that You, Lord Jesus Christ, will spiritually, mentally, emotionally physically and financially bless and protect me. Dear Lord Jesus Christ please help me and break every curse that has ever been spoken over me. Now I ask you Lord Jesus Christ to bless me as I am calling in blessings from the North, South, East, and west in Jesus Christ's name I pray. Amen.

Father in Heaven I ask in Jesus Christ's name that the spirit of Adrammelech, which is the spirit that drives people to commit human sacrifices, is bound up and it will not be allowed to operate anywhere near my home that I live in or the city or town I live in. Please Father, in Jesus Christ's name, send this spirit back to where it came from and In Jesus Christ's name I pray that this spirit will not be able to operate in any way near where I live. In Jesus Christ's name. Amen

In Jesus Christ's name I come against all mystical curses, spells or wives tales; curses you have no power or authority to be near me or come against me. I send you back right to where you come from and in Jesus Christ's name I ask in Jesus Christ's name the power you have and hold on to will be broken, destroyed and crushed in Jesus Christ's name I pray. Amen.

Now I ask Father that you will bless me and bring forth mighty blessings in my life because of evil being spoken against me in Jesus Christ's name amen.

In Jesus Christ's name I come against the false god called Allah which is the god of the Muslim religion. I ask Lord Jesus Christ that this false god and evil religion will not be able to advance any further and you would bind up these false teaching and beliefs. Please Lord Jesus Christ open up the hearts and minds of these people and show them, Lord Jesus Christ, Your awesomeness and reveal to them just how much You love them, in Jesus Christ's name I pray. Amen.

In Jesus Christ's name I bind up all Familiar spirits, Ancestral spirits, and Generation spirits, you are no longer allowed to operate around me and I come against you in the name of Jesus Christ. I come against all your demonic plans and I come against all your demonic insights. In Jesus Christ's name you no longer will be able to operate or gain any type of insight about me because I am covered by the blood of Jesus Christ and in Jesus Christ's name I was bought by the blood of the lamb. Now I ask Lord Jesus Christ to push back the enemy and have mighty blesses be poured out on me in Jesus name. Amen.

In Jesus Christ's name, I ask Lord Jesus Christ to please release a fresh new anointing and let there be a whole new level of Apostolic warfare released in my church and in the churches surrounding this area I live in, plus release this powerful anointing in Churches, for example Churches in Dallas, Texas or Seattle, Washington. Now Lord Jesus Christ raise up your children to walk in this powerful anointing and help them to continue to walk in humility. In Jesus Christ's name I ask that these things be done according to your perfect will, in Jesus Christ's name. Amen.

In Jesus Christ's name I bind up the demonic powers of Astrology and I ask, You, Lord Jesus Christ that these people would be deeply convicted of their sins and they would seek the living God and no longer seek answers from the stars. Please Lord Jesus take the blinders off of these people and help them see You, Lord Jesus Christ. Please Lord Jesus I pray that people who are lost and blind have an encounter with You, in Jesus Christ's name I ask these things. Amen

My Father in Heaven please help those that claim to be into Atheism to see that You are the true and almighty living God. Please loving Father help people to see that You are who You say You are. Father please touch all these people and help them experience your loving hand, here are the names of those that don't believe that I know, now write down on a separate piece of paper all those that aren't saved and pray this prayer.

In Jesus Christ's name I bind up the demonic spirits that keep this person in bondage from receiving the power and knowledge and proof that God is real and He really loves them, in Jesus Christ's name I pray. Amen.

In Jesus Christ's name I bind up all attendant spirits and I come against you in Jesus Christ's name and I come against the plans you have and I speak to you right now in the name of Jesus Christ and I come against your plans and I ask that all your plans will be ripped apart, broken and crushed in Jesus Christ's name. I pray that there will be a fresh new anointing over my life and there would be mighty breakthroughs coming into my life and I would see the manifestations of the blessings of God cover my life. In Jesus Christ's name I ask these prayers and I plead the blood over these prayers. Amen.

I come against the spirit of addiction and I ask You, Lord Jesus, please forgive my ancestors, grandparents, parents and/or myself for allowing this spirit to dictate their lives.

Father in Heaven I ask that you will break the power of addiction and let there be liberty from all addictions. Father in Heaven I know you didn't create me to be dependent on anything, so please Lord Jesus I ask you to push back the enemy and help me walk in the power, authority and freedom in Jesus Christ and I ask You Lord Jesus help me walk in Your power and authority. In Jesus name I pray. Amen.

Father in Heaven I humbly come before You and I ask You to please forgive me for speaking curses, claiming I was speaking prayers. Father if I am not asking someone to draw closer to You, Your ways, or Your decrees, or I am not speaking life but death I am being used by the enemy to do his evil deeds, so please Father convict not only my heart but the heart of others when it comes to prayer, if we are not lined up with the word of God we are being used by Satan to do his evil deeds. So please Father in Heaven continually remind me to speak life even if it is an enemy of mine. In Jesus Christ's name I pray. Amen.

Dear heavenly Father, I ask in Jesus Christ's name that the power of the living God shall pierce the magic circles, secret places and expose the watch towers. Please Heavenly Father, I pray that even when someone paints, draws or makes a pentagram in anyway the power and blood of Jesus Christ shall bring down all demonic powers and authorities and the power of the pentagram shall be bound up no matter where it was painted or drawn and casted down and sent back where it came from. Now thank you Lord Jesus Christ for pulling down all strongholds and bringing every evil and wicked thing into captivity and ending them back where they came from. I praise you Lord Jesus Christ for being so awesome and wonderful. Amen.

Now I seal all my prayers in the Blood of the Lamb and in the power of the Holy Ghost.

Father in Heaven, I ask right now in Jesus Christ's name that all the channels between psychics and spirits or between mediums and spirits and all channels will be disrupted and not one person in my city or town operating under a satanic gift of channeling will be able to operate. Heavenly Father, that all lines of communication shall become confused and nothing that anyone who is working under evil influence shall be able to operate right now in Jesus Christ's name I pray. Amen.

Father in Heaven, I ask right now that you would break and crush a person seeing and feeling the energies of a crystal if it is a satanic or an occult ritual, I ask Father please break the powers of a crystal ball of fortune tellers. Please Father in Heaven remove the spirit of control, heaviness and oppression off their lives and give them a heart to know You, In Jesus Christ's mighty name and in His blood I pray. Amen

In Jesus Christ's name I come against the Python, Father in Heaven bind up the workings of this spirit right now and I demand in the name of Jesus be gone, you have no authority being in this place and you have no right being here, so in Jesus Christ's name I come against you and I rebuke you, be gone now and do not come back in Jesus Christ's name. Father in Heaven may Your power and authority reign in this place. Awesome God I love you and I praise Your holy name. Amen.

Dear Heavenly Father I humble myself and come against all demonic spirits that are trying to destroy me or my business. God all mighty, in the name of Jesus Christ, I ask that You would break the power of any and all territory spirits or tutelary spirits. I ask Heavenly Father to please forgive my parents, grandparents and my ancestors of all wrong, evil and wicked doings. I ask Heavenly Father that You would break all generational curses and please give me and my children full access to Your blessings, power and authority in Jesus Christ's name.

Father in Heaven I long to know You and my heart cries out to You, so please allow me to encounter a deepness with You and Father may You give me and my children a heart to know You. Amen. And now I plead the Blood of Jesus Christ over my life, mind, ears, being, heart, soul, and finances. Thank you Father in Heaven for allowing me to know You. amen. In Jesus Christ's mighty name I pray. Amen

I come against the spirit of Condemnation in the name of Jesus Christ, there is no condemnation and I am free, yes as I shout out freedom my chains are being broken and my walls are crashing down. I am so excited about my new life in Christ and I am now walking in the power, authority and love in Christ and I ask please Lord Jesus Christ help me daily to walk in this new life of Freedom. Amen

In Jesus Christ's name I come against the spirit of oppression, you have no legal right to bind up anyone or any place, so right now in Jesus Christ's name I speak life and life more abundantly over this person or business and I ask Father in Heaven tear down all demonic powers and in Jesus Christ's name I ask Father in Heaven to push back the enemy and don't allow the enemy to advance at all any-where in this person's life or their business. Now Father please let this person or business experience supernatural break through and may Your most Holy name be lifted up, may people shout from the roof tops just how awesome and wonderful their living and loving God is amen. And may the name of Jesus Christ be highly exalted.

In Jesus Christ's name I come against the spirit of doubt, offense, disbelief, self-pity, murder, and hopelessness. Father I need Your help, these spirits seem to be surrounding me everywhere and they are consuming me and I ask that You would please help me fight these demonic attacks and help me walk more like Jesus Christ, so I can walk in humility love, compassion, mercy, understanding and faith fullness. I am so deeply sorry Heavenly Father that I am so self-centered and I am constantly thinking about my pains, hurts and who hasn't been there for me. Lord Jesus consume me in Your presence and may You help me learn how to walk and talk more like You. Father in Heaven please give me the mind of Christ and help me to see that there's a dying world on their way to hell that need Your help. So in Jesus Christ's name I ask Lord Jesus transform me into being like You and help me to walk in Your ways and I ask these things in Jesus Christ's name. Amen

BREAKING FREEMASONRY

"Father in Heaven you are the only true God. You are the Creator of Heaven and earth; I come to you in the name of Jesus Christ your Son, I come as a sinner seeking forgiveness and cleansing from all sins committed against you. I renounce all sins from my parents, grandparents and ancestors. I ask You Father to forgive all my ancestors, parents and grandparents for the effects of their sins on my children and me. I confess and renounce all of my own sins. I renounce and rebuke Satan and every spiritual power of his affecting my family and me.

I renounce and forsake all involvement in Freemasonry or any other lodge or craft by my ancestor's parents, grandparents and myself. I renounce Baphomet, the Spirit of Antichrist and the curse of the Luciferian doctrine. I renounce the idolatry, blasphemy, secrecy and deception of Masonry at every level. I specifically renounce the love of position, power, the love of money, greed, and the pride. I renounce all the fears that held me, my parents, grandparents or ancestors to Masons or Luciferians.

I renounce every position held in the lodge by any of my ancestors, grandparents or myself. I renounce the calling of any man "Master", for Jesus Christ is my only Master and Lord and He forbids anyone else having that title. I renounce the entrapping of others into Masonry, and observing the helplessness of others during the rituals. I renounce the effects of Masonry passed on to me through any female ancestor who felt distrusted and rejected by her husband as he entered and attended any lodge and refused to tell her of his secret activities.

I renounce the Hoodwink, the blindfold, and its effects on emotions and eyes, including all confusion, fear of the dark, fear of the light, and fear of sudden noises. I renounce the secret word BOAZ and all it means. I renounce the mixing and mingling of truth and error and the blasphemy of this degree of Masonry. I renounce the noose around the neck, the fear of choking and also every spirit causing asthma, hay fever, emphysema or any other breathing difficulty. I renounce the compass point, sword or spear held against the breast, the fear of death by stabbing pain and the fear of heart attack from this degree.

In the name of Jesus Christ I now pray for healing of... (The throat, vocal cords, nasal passages, sinus, bronchial tubes etc.) And for healing of the speech area, and the release of the Word of God to me and through me and my family. I cut off emotional hardness, apathy, indifference, unbelief, and deep anger from my family and me.

In the name of Jesus Christ I pray for the healing of the chest/lung/heart area and also for the healing of my emotions, and ask to be made sensitive to the Holy Spirit of God.

I renounce the Spirit of Death from the blows to the head enacted as ritual murder, the fear of death, false martyrdom, fear of violent gang attack, assault or rape; and the helplessness of this degree. I renounce the falling into the coffin or stretcher involved in the ritual of murder. I renounce the false resurrection of this degree because only Jesus Christ is the Resurrection and the Life! I also renounce the blasphemous kissing of the Bible on a Witchcraft oath. I cut off all spirits of death, witchcraft and deception and in the name of Jesus Christ I pray for the healing of the stomach, gall bladder, womb, liver and any other organs of my body affected by Masonry.

I renounce the claim that the death of Jesus Christ was a 'dire calamity', and also the deliberate mockery and twisting of the Christian doctrine of the Atonement. I renounce the blasphemy and rejection of the deity of Jesus Christ. I cut off all these curses and their effects on my family and me in the name of Jesus Christ, and I pray for healing of the brain, the mind etc.

-------BREAK ALL SECRET CURSES -------

I renounce all the other oaths taken in the rituals of every other degree and the curses involved. I renounce all other lodges and secret societies such as Prince Hall Freemasonry, Mormonism, The Order of Amaranth, Odd fellows, Buffaloes, Druids, Foresters, Orange, Elks, Moose and Eagles Lodges, the Ku Klux Klan, The Grange, the Woodmen of the World, Riders of the Red Robe, the Knights of Pythias, the Mystic Order of the Veiled Prophets of the Enchanted Realm, the Women's Orders of the Eastern Star and of the White Shrine of Jerusalem, The Girls' order of the Daughters of the Eastern Star, the International Orders of Job's Daughters, Daughters of the Night and Mothers of Darkness

I renounce the All-Seeing Third Eye of Freemasonry or Horus in the forehead and its pagan and occult symbolism. I renounce all false communions taken, all mockery of the redemptive work of Jesus Christ on the cross of Calvary, all unbelief, confusion and depression and all worship of Lucifer as God. I renounce and forsake the lie of Freemasonry that man is not sinful, but merely imperfect and so he can redeem himself through good works. I rejoice that the Bible states that I cannot do a single thing to earn my salvation, but that I can only be saved by grace through faith in Jesus Christ and what He accomplished on the Cross of Calvary.

I renounce all fear of insanity, anguish, death wishes, suicide and death in the name of Jesus Christ. Jesus Christ conquered death and He alone holds the keys of death and hell and I rejoice that He holds my life in His hands now. He came to give me life abundantly and eternally, and I believe His promises.

I renounce all anger, hatred, murderous thoughts, revenge, retaliation, spiritual apathy, false religion, all unbelief, especially unbelief in the Holy Bible as God's Word, and all compromise of God's Word. I renounce all spiritual searching into false religions and all striving to please God, I rest in the knowledge that I have found my Lord and Savior Jesus Christ, and that He has found me.

I will burn all objects in my possession which connect me with all lodges and or cultic organizations, including Masonry, Witchcraft and Mormonism and all regalia, aprons, books of rituals, rings and other jewelry. I renounce the effects of these or other objects of Masonry, such as the compass, the square, the noose or the blindfold, have had on me or my family, in Jesus Name

Now dear, Father God, I ask humbly for the blood of Jesus Christ, your Son, to cleanse me from all these sins I have confessed and renounced, to cleanse my spirit, my soul, my mind, my emotions and every part of my body which has been affected by these sins. In Jesus' name. Amen

Father, in the name of Jesus Christ Your Son, please forgive me for practicing meditation, trying to find peace of inner self when I should have been looking and seeking for Jesus Christ. Forgive me Father for practicing new age and eastern religion concepts; You are the only one that can offer true peace Lord Jesus Christ. There are no other ways to finding God the Father, everyone must seek You Lord Jesus Christ, You truly are the only way. Amen

Father in Heaven please I call upon You now in this dreadful hour, I feel so isolated, abandoned, hopeless, insecure, depressed, lonely and all alone as if no one cares or understands. Please Father I am crying out to You with all my strength to please break this oppression over my life, please every ounce of me is pleading with You, my loving Father to take away this oppression from me. I don't want to be under this oppression for one more second, please Father in Heaven, every part of me is feeling crushed and all I can do is sit and cry, asking why must I endure this one more second, Please now Father come to my rescue in Jesus Christ's Holy name and turn my tears and sorrow into praising and shouting just how awesome my loving Father is, in Jesus Christ's name, sealed in the blood. Amen

Father in Heaven, so many are looking for a way to cope with all the pain, stress, hurt, loneliness or fearful things happening today. Sexually transmitted diseases amongst people over the age of 50 has gone way up, leaders of churches and pastors leaving the ministry, so many are having an affair, so many are turning to drugs, prescriptions, turning to alcohol, turning to gambling, turning to sex or porn, so many are thinking if I just get into a religious group or join a cult then I will find hope, so many are leaving their spouse, so many are becoming gay, plus so many are now wanting to go to a hypnosis seminar, so many are turning their backs on You Lord Jesus Christ wanting to find joy, peace, an escape. But Lord Jesus there's only hope in You, there's only peace in You, so I am crying out please, yes my Lord and Savior, please forgive us of our wicked and evil sins. Please Lord Almighty forgive us for our stupidity, ignorance, pride, selfish ambitions, selfish desires and self-centeredness. In Jesus Christ's name I pray for mercy. Amen.

Father in the name of Jesus Christ forgive us for drawing pictures and painting pictures of lustful, seductive and perverted angels. God Almighty we have left the knowledge that You God, you are a holy and just God full of purity and righteousness. God forgive us for turning something so holy, pure and loving into such perversion and wickedness. In Jesus Christ's name give us a heart for the things of God. Amen.

Father in Heaven forgive us please for worshiping Angels. God you are the one and only we should worship only You. God convict our hearts of such evil and give us a heart to know You and to worship You only. I ask Lord thy God to please call each and every one of us to seek and know the heart of God. God forgive me and forgive this nation for turning its back on You. So I ask that this prayer and all my prayers be sealed in the blood, power, authority in Jesus Christ's name I pray. Amen

SPIRITUAL WARFARE SCRIPTURES

Exodus 14:14
The Lord will fight for you, and you shall hold your peace."

Exodus 23:27-28
"I will send My fear before you, I will cause confusion among all the people to whom you come, and will make all your enemies turn their backs to you. 28 And I will send hornets before you, which shall drive out the Hivite, the Canaanite, and the Hittite from before you.

Leviticus 19:31
Give no regard to mediums and familiar spirits; do not seek after them, to be defiled by them: I am the Lord your God.

Joshua 1:9
Have I not commanded you? Be strong and of good courage; do not be afraid, nor be dismayed, for the Lord your God is with you wherever you go

1 Kings 18:28
So they cried aloud, and cut themselves, as was their custom, with knives and lances, until the blood gushed out on them.

2 Kings 15:16
Then from Tirzah, Menahem attacked Tiphsah, all who were there, and its territory. Because they did not surrender, therefore he attacked it. All the women there who were with child he ripped open.

Psalm 107:14
He brought them out of darkness and the shadow of death, And broke their chains in pieces.

Isaiah 40:31
But those who wait on the Lord Shall renew their strength; They shall mount up with wings like eagles, They shall run and not be weary, They shall walk and not faint.

Jeremiah 24:7
Then I will give them a heart to know Me, that I am the Lord; and they shall be My people, and I will be their God, for they shall return to Me with their whole heart

Matthew 11:12
And from the days of John the Baptist until now the kingdom of heaven suffers violence, and the violent take it by force.

Ezekiel 22:30
So I sought for a man among them who would make a wall, and stand in the gap before Me on behalf of the land, that I should not destroy it; but I found no one

Luke 5:5
But Simon answered and said to Him, "Master, we have toiled all night and caught nothing; nevertheless at Your word I will let down the net."

Luke 6:46
"But why do you call Me 'Lord, Lord,' and not do the things which I say?

John 10:10
The thief does not come except to steal, and to kill, and to destroy. I have come that they may have life, and that they may have it more abundantly.

John 12:32
And I, if I am lifted up from the earth, will draw all peoples to Myself."

Acts 5:16
Also a multitude gathered from the surrounding cities to Jerusalem, bringing sick people and those who were tormented by unclean spirits, and they were all healed.

Acts 16:17-18
This girl followed Paul and us, and cried out, saying, "These men are the servants of the Most High God, who proclaim to us the way of salvation."

18 And this she did for many days. But Paul, greatly annoyed, turned and said to the spirit, "I command you in the name of Jesus Christ to come out of her." And he came out that very hour.

Romans 8:1
There is therefore now no condemnation to those who are in Christ Jesus,[a] who do not walk according to the flesh, but according to the Spirit

Romans 8:37
Yet in all these things we are more than conquerors through Him who loved us.

Ephesians 3:14-20
For this reason I bow my knees to the Father of our Lord Jesus Christ,[a]

15 from whom the whole family in heaven and earth is named,

16 that He would grant you, according to the riches of His glory, to be strengthened with might through His Spirit in the inner man,

17 that Christ may dwell in your hearts through faith; that you, being rooted and grounded in love,

18 may be able to comprehend with all the saints what is the width and length and depth and height.

19 to know the love of Christ which passes knowledge; that you may be filled with all the fullness of God.

20 Now to Him who is able to do exceedingly abundantly above all that we ask or think, according to the power that works in us

Mark 8:17
But Jesus, being aware of it, said to them, (Why do you reason) because you have no bread? Do you not yet perceive nor understand? Is your heart still[HYPERLINK "https://www.biblegateway.com/passage/?search=mark+8%3A17&version=NKJV" \l "fen-NKJV-24518a" \t "_blank" \o "See footnote a" a] hardened

Philippians 2:9
Therefore God also has highly exalted Him and given Him the name which is above every name,

Philippians 4:13
I can do all things through Christ[HYPERLINK "https://www.biblegateway.com/passage/?search=Philippians+4&version=NKJV" \l "fen-NKJV-29456b" \t "_blank" \o "See footnote b" b] who strengthens me

Colossians 1:13-14
He has delivered us from the power of darkness and conveyed us into the kingdom of the Son of His love, 14 in whom we have redemption through His blood,[HYPERLINK "https://www.bible-gateway.com/passage/?search=Colossians+1&version=NKJV" \l "fen-NKJV-29480c" \o "See footnote c" \t "_blank" c] the forgiveness of sins.

Colossians 2:15
Having disarmed principalities and powers, He made a public spectacle of them, triumphing over them in it.

2 Corinthians 5:17
Therefore, if anyone is in Christ, he is a new creation; old things have passed away; behold, all things have become new.

2 Corinthians 11:3-4
But I fear, lest somehow, as the serpent deceived Eve by his craftiness, so your minds may be corrupted from the simplicity[HYPERLINK "https://www.biblegateway.com/passage/?search=2+Corinthians+11%3A3-4+&version=NKJV" \l "fen-NKJV-28993a" \t "_blank" \o "See footnote a" a] that is in Christ.

4 For if he who comes preaches another Jesus whom we have not preached, or if you receive a different spirit which you have not received, or a different gospel which you have not accepted—you may well put up with it!

2 Corinthians 11:14
And no wonder! For Satan himself transforms himself into an angel of light.

1 Timothy 4:1
Now the Spirit expressly says that in latter times some will depart from the faith, giving heed to deceiving spirits and doctrines of demons

2 Timothy 1:7
For God has not given us a spirit of fear, but of power and of love and of a sound mind.

2 Timothy 3:1-7
But know this, that in the last days perilous times will come:

2 For men will be lovers of themselves, lovers of money, boasters, proud, blasphemers, disobedient to parents, unthankful, unholy,

3 unloving, unforgiving, slanderers, without self-control, brutal, despisers of good,

4 traitors, headstrong, haughty, lovers of pleasure rather than lovers of God, 5 having a form of godliness but denying its power. And from such people turn away!

6 For of this sort are those who creep into households and make captives of gullible women loaded down with sins, led away by various lusts,

7 always learning and never able to come to the knowledge of the truth.

2 Timothy 4:18
And the Lord will deliver me from every evil work and preserve me for His heavenly kingdom. To Him be glory forever and ever. Amen!

Titus 1:16
They profess to know God, but in works they deny Him, being abominable, disobedient, and disqualified for every good work.

Hebrews 11:6
But without faith it is impossible to please Him, for he who comes to God must believe that He is, and that He is a re-warder of those who diligently seek Him.

James 3:16
For where envy and self-seeking exist, confusion and every evil thing are there.

James 4:7
Therefore submit to God. Resist the devil and he will flee from you.

1 Peter 2:24
who Himself bore our sins in His own body on the tree, that we, having died to sins, might live for righteousness—by whose stripes you were healed.

1 John 3:8
He who sins is of the devil, for the devil has sinned from the beginning. For this purpose the Son of God was manifested, that He might destroy the works of the devil.

Revelation 12:11
And they overcame him by the blood of the Lamb and by the word of their testimony, and they did not love their lives to the death

Revelation 16:14
For they are spirits of demons, performing signs, which go out to the kings of the earth and[a] of the whole world, to gather them to the battle of that great day of God Almighty.

Revelation 21:8
But the cowardly, unbelieving, [HYPERLINK "https://www.biblegateway.com/passage/?search=Revelation%20 21:8&version=NKJV" \l "fen-NKJV-31062a" \t "_blank" \o "See footnote a" a] abominable, murderers, sexually immoral, sorcerers, idolaters, and all liars shall have their part in the lake which burns with fire and brimstone, which is the second death."